I0417238

FRATERNAL
FANTASY

GARRET R. JORDAN

This book, and everything else that I do, is for my momma... I Love you.

PART 1

It's true. I had the perfect life. I had the life every female wanted. A great job, no kids yet, a loving boyfriend, and a degree in English Literature. I'm 26, and I teach English composition at a local high school, here in Mississippi.

I met my boyfriend Rakim during an Anatomy & Physiology lab assignment my junior year in college. Let's just say, it was lust at first sight.

I remember it like it was yesterday....

"Do you already have a partner?" I heard a deep voice ask me from behind.

"Umm no, not yet, but..." I began to explain before turning around and becoming so captivated by the most gorgeous black man I'd ever seen on campus.

"No, not at all, here, you can sit here..." I immediately moved my MK purse and extra set of goggles to the floor, to make room for him. He made himself comfortable and began to remove his jacket. I glanced at his profile and noticed how clean cut he was, and the way his lips protruded from his face. Long black eyelashes, nice cheek bones and a perfect smile to top it all off. Damn, he was prettier than me.

"Cool, I'm Rakim by the way..." He said, flashing all his beautiful teeth and reaching his hand towards me, to shake mine.

"I'm Destiny." I said, returning the hospitality.

I took a deep breath, and inhaled the most intriguing scent I'd ever smelled on anyone.

"You smell amazing..." The words slipped out of my mouth before I even noticed it.

"Ha, thanks, it's Armani." He responded, looking at me slightly crazy.

"And that's Euphoria you're wearing, right?" He asked.

I smiled politely, and tried to remember the name on the box of perfume my mom had just given me the other day.

"Y-y-yeah, I think so, my mom actually picked it out for me." I responded with embarrassment.

"Moms has good taste, I must say. Umm excuse me for being so blunt, but you're not from around here are you?" He asked politely. And the fact that he added an (S) to mom, was different and grammatically incorrect but sexy.

"No, I'm actually from DC, but I've lived here in Mississippi for most of my life, what about you?"

"Yes ma'am, born and raised right here baby!" He said with excitement while slowing lifting his sleeve to display his Mississippi tattoo.

That was one thing I never understood about brothers. Clearly your country ass is from here, no need to stamp yourself to prove your consistency to your hometown.

"Cute..." I responded.

"Okay! Less talking, more working!" Dr. Wilson said aloud as if he was directing the statement to us.

I enjoyed the way Rakim was heavily respectful. He responded to me constantly with no ma'am, and yes ma'am, although I appeared to be younger than him.

After Dr. Wilson's announcement, he started to work diligently, until we were the first ones complete with our assignment.

Rakim is about 6'4, 180 lbs., with big hands, and the size of his Jordan's looked like they had to be specially ordered. His skin was jet black, like he had to have been from down south or from an island I couldn't pronounce. He wore a low-cut fade, with deep waves that shined from the lighting in the class room. His nails were manicured, and I could see his veins going up his forearm, as if he masturbated for a living.

"Lord, this man is fine." I thought to myself.

"Done!" He said proudly, exposing all 32 teeth!

We both removed our goggles and raised our hand, as if we would receive a prize for being the first students finished.

"Bring me your lab reports and I'll see you guys next Tuesday." Dr. Wilson said while lowering his glasses.

The thought of waiting another week to see him, made me sad.

"Look, I've never done this before, but I have this weird feeling about you. It's almost like I know you from somewhere, you think I can take you out for dinner and a movie sometime?" He asked with a look of uncertainty.

I smiled.

"You didn't even ask me if I was single though." I said flirtatiously.

"I'm certain that you're single Ms. Destiny?" He responded with confidence.

"Oh really? How is that?" I asked.

"Because any man dating you, would be a damn fool not to marry right away. Especially with brothers, like myself, waking around campus." He replied.

I liked his confidence. Before I responded I noticed the colors he was wearing. The color of his binder and the smooth talking that would eventually lead to some innocent school girl, knocked up somewhere.

"Nupe?" I asked with one eyebrow raised.

"Is it that obvious?" He said while trying to contain his smile.

One thing I'd picked up around campus was the fraternity brothers. They were all different but one thing they all had in common was the ease to talk any female right out of her Victoria Secrets. But fuck it, I thought to myself, I wasn't wearing panties anyway.

"When are you free?" I asked.

"Tonight, so I'll pick you up around 7, be ready. You stay on campus or university apartments?" He asked, without even checking if I were free.

"Apartment, University Edge. And make it 6:30, I can't be out too late." I replied, just to feel like I had some say so in the matter.

I collected my belongings and headed for the door.

"I'll see you soon Ms. Destiny."

I felt my body quiver, whenever he said my name.

To Be Continued.

PART 2

I walked through my apartment doors and was immediately greeted by the sweet smell of warm vanilla sugar. I had obtained this weird obsession with the scented melted waxes, so my apartment was stained with the smells of vanilla, cinnamon and apples. I opened my room door, took off my boots and laid down to regroup my thoughts and possibly masturbate before my date.

I'd learned that masturbating before a date would reduce the tendency to sleep with the person by 80%. I fixed my laptop up and begin to remove my jeans when...

"Roommate! Let's go have lunch somewhere, I'm thinking Mexican! 2 for 1 margaritas? And them cheap tacos you like so much? Come on." I could always count on my roommate, Briana, to ruin a wet dream, literally.

"Eww, what you doing?" She asked with a look of disgust on her face.

"Nothing Bri! Damn!" I replied with frustration.

"Ummmm, you on your period, why the attitude chick?" She asked while making herself comfortable at the foot of my bed.

"I'm fine, my bad... How was school today?" I asked to lower the tension.

"Good... Did you remember I needed your help with that paper tonight, so you still got me right?" She peeped up from her phone to inquire my response.

"Shit, Bri I'm sorry I forgot! And I made plans tonight, when is it due?" I asked.

"Plans? Ha, with who?" She asked as if it were some type of joke.

"Some dude I met today in Lab, it's just dinner and a movie, so don't look at me like that." I responded.

"Roommate what?! When, where, tell me all about him!" By this time she had made her way from the foot of my bed, to 10 inches from my face.

"Some dude named Rakim, I, ummmm..." She put her hand over my mouth and I darted my eyes to her direction.

"Rakim Abdul?" She asked with her eyes wide open as if he was a mass murderer!

"Destiny that is the most beautiful man on campus girllllll! And he Muslim! Now you know us Christians but it almost seems forbidden to be tapping that Muslim Mandingo! Did you touch it?"

"Bri! Stop! EW, I just met him and I'm not trying to marry him or sex him, it's just a movie dang! Calm down girl!" I explained to her. One thing about Bri, is she was a southern belle, with the mouth of an old black church woman!

"And how do you know his religion?" I asked, stopping her in the middle of her rant.

"I guessed it." She replied and we both burst out laughing!

"Chick you stupid!"

A couple hours passed and then it was time for me to get cute. But not too cute.

I'd just gotten a sew-in done, so I just needed to flat iron my hair and put some make up on. I'm 5'6, 145 pounds, 32-26-39 measurement with a 32C. I'm all natural, even my hair but virgin Brazilian bundles have become my best friend. I'm guess, I'm somewhat of a dime. But I have a hard time convincing myself that I am.

For the date I decided to wear some cute ripped Hollister dark denim jeans, a white V-neck and a red blazer, with my black boots. It was cute, but not overly sexy.

I made it to the Cinema theatre around 6:25, and sent him a text to check on his whereabouts.

At exactly 6:30 on the dot I was frightened by a knock on my window. I let it down...

"Destiny you are something else..."

"Why you say that?"

"The men in my family are complete gentleman, I would've really liked to pick you up from your apartment..."

"I don't know you just yet to be hoping in your car, slow down turbo..." I said jokingly.

He opened my door and put his hand out to lift me out of my black, chromed out, Toyota Camry.

"Nice whip D."

"Thanks..."

We made our way into the movies and I enjoyed being with such a gentleman. Opened every door, paid for everything, and continuously said no ma'am, and yes ma'am as if I were his elder.

After the movie, "The Help," we were intrigued in conversation about black culture and shared numerous stories of our childhood. Over endless pasta and salad at Olive Garden.

I was stunned out how intelligent he was. And how motivated his was about changing the community around him. He went on and on about creating boys and girls clubs and being a teacher, coach, etc., all to inspire the minds of your youth.

"What's your religion?" He asked the question I dreaded because of Briana's crazy ass.

"I'm Muslim." He responded. "And you?"

"I could tell you were Muslim by your eagerness to pray and plethora of questions about the pork." I responded, "But I'm a Christian"

He raised an eyebrow, "oh really? Okay, that's cool. Anyone adamant about proclaiming her faith, no matter the religion is okay with me."

But I sensed, that was a lie. I didn't know much about Muslim men but I was sure, it wouldn't be the end of the subject as long as we continued to converse.

We got back to our cars and I closed my door and let my window down.

"So Ms. Destiny, I know you may so no, but I would do anything to kiss you one time, could I do that?" He asked respectfully.

He licked his lips and I felt my pussy quiver.

"I really enjoyed myself, but let's not kiss on the first date." I responded.

"So there will be more ma'am" he asked.

"I sure as hell hope so." I rolled up my window and couldn't wait to call Bri!

To Be Continued...

PART 3

By the time I made it home, the only thing I could think about was the lasting scent of the fine man I had just left. When I got inside, there was a note on the bar, from Bri.

"Going to Brittany's for the night, text me when you make it home. Love you, and I can't wait to hear about the date with Rakim."

I chuckled to myself and went to my room to masturbate in overtime. Pornhub had honestly become my boyfriend! It was hard being a virtuous woman. I had needs, but they would just have to be satisfied by old faithful, my vibrator.

I softly grazed my fingertips across my hard nipples and laid down slowly over my bed. I had no panties on just a crop top t-shirt and my eye glasses. I turned the computer on "Roc & Shay" from Pornhub and eased my hand from my breast, down my torso, and gently caressed my clit.....

And then I blacked out...

-Tacara

Hello everyone, I'm Tacara. You haven't heard much about me because I only get to come out when Destiny is beyond horny. I only have one mission, and that's to fuck the first eligible bachelor on campus. She knows nothing about me, only the nasty stench and red lipstick smears that she washes away the morning after. It sounds crazy, but I'm normal. Most women have a split personality they know nothing about, and wonder why people call them whores.

This night was particularly special because I watched her interacting with Rakim, but he's not really my type. So I'll let her have him to herself. Kappas & Alphas are fun, but I'm more of the Que or Sigma type. I'll explain later...

I rose up from the bed and took of the hideous crop-top she was wearing. I slipped on some black laced panties and covered myself in an all-black, skin tight, halter mini-skirt. I slightly teased my hair out and added a touch of plum colored lipstick. She only wore basic heels, so I went to the back of her closet to pull out some special red bottom black pumps, and was headed out the door.

I didn't even make it down the steps of my apartment when I was stopped by the scent of masculinity. I was like a bitch in heat.

"Damn lil momma, who are you, I ain't ever seen you before?" I heard a want to-be thug shout from behind as I was walking down the stairs.

I turned around sensually and responded.

The first thing I noticed was his stamp of approval on his chest. There was nothing like the branding on a Que-Dog.

"I'm T. Who the hell are you?" I asked with an attitude.

"I-I-I- I'm Ashton," he responded stumbling over his words, as if he was shocked that I was even acknowledging his presence.

Awkwardly, even people that knew Destiny, didn't know who she was when she was in "Tacara" form. It was something about the way I carried myself or maybe the lack of the big Ray Ban bifocals she always had covering up our beauty.

"Ashton huh? You're kind of cute..."

"Oh really, what you getting into tonight?" He asked while reaching his hand out to greet me.

"Horny, very horny..." I replied. And his eyes got huge.

"Huh, what? So you tryna fuck something huh?"

I lifted my skin tight skirt to show the print of my pussy lips through my black laced panties. I rubbed my index and middle finger across it to imply "yes" to his question.

Ashton had to have been about 6'2, extra bright skin, long sandy-red colored dreads, with tattoos covering 70% of his body. He appeared to have just been outside his apartment to smoke his black and mild, so he was only wearing some black basketball shorts, some purple plaid boxers, long socks, with a pair of Jordan slides on. No shirt.

"Damn... What you tryna do?" He asked while grabbing his dick that was growing larger by the second. I walked up to him, and touched it for myself. It was rock hard. I slowly caressed it through his shorts and watched him trimmer when I rolled my fingertips across the head.

"Come on..." I told him while opening the door to our apartment.

"Hold up, wait, this is Bri's apartment..." He responded. "And my girl ughhh... Fuck it"

"Nigga, shut up and eat this pussy..."

I lifted my body over the bar and slid my skirt up to my stomach, exposing my thighs and panties. He started to look as if he couldn't believe what was about to happen. He slid my panties down as he cuffed the base of my thighs and slowly elevated them to where my pussy was sitting on the bar like a Sunday dinner.

His tongue was so long, I swear I could feel it in my stomach. He took his time stroking and swerving his tongue in every direction. He was damn sure no amateur at what he was doing. He bent down, put my legs over his shoulders and lifted me from the bar and laid me on the carpet. I felt like Tyrese's mom in that movie "Baby Boy."

"You gon let me fuck?" He asked.

"Naw, I wanna fuck you, so lay down..." I responded.

He laid flat on the carpet but sat up on his elbows to see what I was doing. He was so sexy with his dreads falling right above his nipples. I kissed his chest and slid my tongue all the way down his torso until my mouth was fully connected with his dick, which was standing at full attention. I kissed his abs, then his inner thighs, teasing his dick. Then, I sucked it for several minutes until I could taste his pre-cum in the back of my throat. That's when I pulled my skirt completely off, exposing my breast and my wet pussy lips. I grabbed my breast and allowed him to kiss and suck on them, while hunching the shaft of his dick with my warm cat.

I rode the life out of him. I had him moaning and grasping my hips, elevating his ass to thrust and go deeper inside of me. After I had came about 3 times, I took his dick out and beat it until he bust a huge nut all over his own stomach and some on the carpet....

I stood up, to walk him to the door and thank him for the lay, when there was a knock at the door!

"Ashton! Open the fuckin door before I break this bitch down!!!" A female voice yelled!

-Destiny is going to be so mad at me. I thought to myself...

To Be Continued...

PART 4

-Tacara

I put a large t-shirt on and headed for my door. There were a couple extra positive sides to me, I didn't take as much bull shit as Destiny would.

I swung my door open...

"Can I help you?" I asked ever so politely. Sizing her up and down with my eyes.

"Yeah, is Ashton in there?! His homeboy Rhashad said he seen him come in this apartment? So where he at?" She asked with a neck roll, and peeping over my shoulders to get a better view.

I slid my head in the direction to block her view of my dwelling.

"Excuse me bitch, first of all who is Ashton, second of all, what would he be doing here? And lastly, who the fuck are you?!" I asked the series of questions while placing my Brazilian bundles into a pony tail... Just in case!

"I-I-I-ummmm," she began to stamper over her words, not expecting that comeback.

"Ugh-uh-you were just about to get your raggedy ass out of my door way before I beat the breaks off of you!"

"Destiny?" She said squinting her eyes with a puzzled look on her face.

"No bitch, it's Tacara!" I said before slamming the door in her face.

I collected my thoughts from feeling like Mayweather's little sister and was greeted by a soft, wet kiss from Ashton.

"Thank you..." He whispered in relief. I could tell from his tone and the look on his face, she was a worsen ass girlfriend. I softly kissed him back and proceeded for a round two. "Destiny is going to kill me..." I thought to myself.

-Destiny

I woke up the next day with the most disgusting feeling and taste in my mouth. My body was sore and the last thing I remembered was opening my computer screen. I must have had one too many Apple Martinis the night before. I got out of my bed and went to the mirror and was horrified. I barely recognized myself. I looked as if I had just woke up from being a prostitute. EW!

"No more drinking for a while..." I said to myself.

I took a shower, brushed my teeth, flat ironed my hair, and opened my closet to find something to wear. I reached to the side of the closet and there was a skin tight, black, mini skirt with fresh deodorant marks as if it were just worn. I'd never seen it before and was sure Bri hadn't turned into a prostitute overnight. Maybe it was Jaleisa's (one of our other friends).

I got my keys, got my purse, grabbed my laptop bag and was headed off to class. As soon as I opened the door I was greeted with a dozen roses, a small pink envelope and a brown, fuzzy teddy bear.

The note said:
"Words can't explain the way I felt last night. I hope this doesn't freak you out that I took the liberty of finding out where you stay, but I had to find some way to express my generosity from last night. I can't wait to see you again. -Rakim"

I felt my cheeks burning. I was blushing. And yeah, I was slightly freaked out but I was almost positive, all he had to do was ask Bri over Facebook. That girl was determined to marry me off.

I pushed my glasses closer to my face, picked up my roses, placed them in the apartment and continued on with my day. But now, with the biggest smile on my face. I thought about him nonstop!

I made it to Child Developmental Studies, before everyone else as usual. Not only did I adore the class, but my professor, Dr. Bolden had to have been one of the most gorgeous and intellectual men on the planet. It was something about older black men with black frames, button downs tucked in, with a little gray just on the temples of their low cut fades. Hot! Dr. Bolden was well in his 50's, played basketball for USM back in the day, and was married to the Dean of the Education department on campus. My fairy tale life.

"Today we're discussing the Freud's 5 stages of Psychosexual Development, who can tell me what they are?" Dr. Bolden asked aloud and the entire classroom looked in my direction.

That was one thing other students, females in general, disliked about me. I always knew the lesson plans in advance. Professors give us a syllabus for a reason.

My hand went up reluctantly.

"Ah, yes, Ms. Destiny, of course..." Dr. Bolden said with pleasure. He had become use to my quick ability to answer questions and had even offered me a work-study job as his TA.

"Freud's five stages of psychosexual development are the Oral, Anal, Phallic, Latent, and Puberty stages, sir. Oral being the first stage where the child becomes familiarized with his/her mouth... And..." I was interrupted.

"Ha, okay, okay Ms. Destiny, would you mind if I teach my class today?" Dr. Bolden asked sarcastically.

"Sorry, I got a little carried away..." I said as the class chuckled softly at my embarrassment.

As Dr. Bolden continued with his lecture, about Freud's 5 stages, I drifted off into a daydream about my childhood...

(April 8, 1997)

"Destiny! You have 10 minutes to get your narrow behind downstairs for Sunday school!" My mom yelled to me through my bedroom door.

"Momma I'm coming!" I replied

"Don't sass mouth me girl!"

"Yes ma'am..."

After an hour of trying to pick out the perfect Sunday dress, I was greeted with dismay downstairs.

"You can't wear that! You wore that the last first Sunday, go change! And do something with your hair, it looks a mess! And those shoes, Destiny, do I always have to dress you! You have 10 minutes to fix yourself or I'll leave you here and the devil can deal with you!" My mom snapped at me and made me feel like I was the scum of the earth.

I cried on my way to the stairs as I heard her greeting my brothers with praise for always being able to do things on their own.

"Destiny hurry up! Dang!" My brother Devin yelled up the stairs!

"I'm coming!"

I was the outcast of our "Perfect little family." My mom and dad praised both my brothers, Devin & Deshaun, and I was basically an unplanned mistake. I spent most of my time reading books of all kinds! While most kids my age were playing with Barbie dolls, I was trying to figure out Newton's laws of gravity.

Yeah, I was different.

All work, no play but it would pay off some day.

To Be Continued...

PART 5

-Destiny

It was finally Friday and the only thing I could think about were the dinner plans Rakim and I had planned the night before. Since the day he brought me the roses, we'd studied together, text and talked on the phone but absolutely no funny business, I wasn't that type of girl.

"Yesssss honey its going down tonight!" Bri came bursting in my room chanting!

"Girl what? No, we're just having dinner and a couple drinks at Mugshots!" I replied to her while still scrummaging through my closet to find something decent to wear.

"How do you think this would look?" I asked her holding up a blue and white polka dotted dress, with white sequence. "Cute right?"

"Like a damn mess! Go fix your hair and your make up, make yourself look like something, I'll find your outfit." Bri snapped back as she pushed me out of the way to enter my closet.

"Geez okay," I suddenly felt like I was at my mother's houses again.

I turned on Big Sean's- Marvin Gaye and Chardonnay and began to reconstruct my face.

After about 45 minutes of trying to become someone totally different, I walked out of the bathroom excited to show Bri my makeup.

"What did you do different Destiny? It barely look like you washed your damn face! Girl come on here..." She exclaimed while grabbing my by the hand and dragging me back into the bathroom.

It took her less than 30 minutes and I was fabulous! She's ironed my hair out to perfection, arched and shaded my eyebrows lightly, added eyeliner, some burgundy lipstick, dark eyeshadow and some light blush, and I could barely recognize myself. I stood in the mirror and thanked her repeatedly. I didn't look like I was about to work a corner but I definitely looked sexy and seductive.

"Can I still wear my glasses?" I asked nonchalantly.

"Yep, it they go with your outfit, come look..." She responded.

It was a sheer, royal blue, high rise blouse, some tight fitted, short ass white shorts, an off white bra, with some brown wedge sandals.

"Who's wearing that?" I lowered my glasses to get a better look.

"You are!" Bri responded!

"No Bri, I'm not leaving the house like that! No, heck no! I'll look easy or like I'm asking for it!" I shouted across the room waving my hands 'no!'

"Destiny, your last boyfriend was in the 7th grade with big headed ass John! You never get out, you masturbate and read sex novels religiously! You need a life, you need a boyfriend! Hell, you need to be asking for it!" Bri responded without a smile on her face.

I held up the blouse...

"What about my stomach?"

"Your slim ass look like you need a burger! Put the damn shirt on!"

I put on the skimpy outfit and I must say, I looked damn good. Bri had convinced me last year to get a tattoo on my lower pelvic bone and you could see it peaking above the rim of the shorts. I looked cute, seductive, hell, I looked hot!

"You go girl! Selfie time!" Bri said, holding out her phone before I left the house.

I got my keys and my purse and was on my way out the door, when a voice stopped me in the living room.

"It's about time Ms. Destiny and might I say, you look absolutely amazing baby girl. Excuse my language but damn!" Rakim had been waiting in the living room without me knowing. Bri's extra sneaky ass!

I blushed.

"Thanks Rakim, you look really nice as well..." I replied reaching out to give him a hug.

"Should I take my glasses off?" I asked looking up at him.

"No ma'am, I love your glasses, you ready?" He reached his hand to hold mine and my knees got weak.

"I'm ready..."

At dinner we both got mushroom, Swiss burgers and I almost added bacon to mine but didn't out of respect. Everything about Rakim was charming and interesting, and everywhere he went, people spoke and acknowledge his presence. Not to mention, all the other beautiful women in the room, but he was only interested in me. I felt so good to be with him.

"So tell me about your family, you always ask about mine but leave out so many details about yours... I want to know more!" I said with the biggest smile on my face.

"Okay, okay, well as you know I'm a Mississippi man, and so was my dad."

"Was?" I asked, interrupting his story already.

"Yeah, he passed away when my brother and I were 12.."

"I'm so sorry..."

"Its fine, it's fine. In those 12 years he installed everything we needed in order to provide for my sister and mom. My twin brother Hakeem is slightly different from me and stresses me out constantly, but I would die if he ever stopped breathing." He said with a look of sincerity.

"Wait, what? You're joking, so there's 2 of you?" I asked and almost choked on my French fries at the thought of there being another man that fine.

"Ha-ha, yeah, we're identical. More now, than we used to be."

"Do you have a picture of him?" I asked eager to get a look at him.

"I do, but I do you one better, I've been telling him about you, and he'll actually be here tomorrow. You want to meet him then?" He asked.

"I would love to."

He continued telling me about his past, his family and his future, and I enjoyed every minute of it.

After a couple hours passed, the restaurant had become deserted. We were literally the only people in the building. We had already paid, but just felt like sitting and talking.

"We should probably go..." I whispered to him as we both looked around to see the servers sweeping around our feet.

"You're probably right..." Rakim replied, standing up and holding out his hand to walk me out.

We got in the car and something so strange began to come over me. I figured I may have just been lightheaded, or slightly tipsy but the feeling didn't go away after a few minutes.

"Baby you okay?" Rakim asked grasping my hand across the car.

"I'm fine, I just feel..." My mind went blank, and I blacked out.

-Tacara

"I feel fine, I just probably should go lie down." I replied to the question that was intended for Destiny.

I immediately took them damn glasses off because I couldn't see shit with those things on. I looked at his bad ass car and was quite impressed with Destiny's accomplishment with finding him.

"Not bad..." I said aloud on accident.

"What was that baby?" He asked.

"Oh nothing baby," I responded politely and dignified, which are too things I'm not.

We pulled up to the girls' apartment and he got out to open my door.

"I got it..." I replied before realizing I didn't want to ruin whatever he and Destiny have going on.

That's the thing about us. I loved her dearly, but I just couldn't express myself the way I wanted to without tarnishing her beauty queen reputation.

"Ummm okay, thanks for the night..." I waved politely trying to be cute.

"Wait, no hug, no kiss?" He asked and for the first time I got nervous. See, I wasn't used to coming out whenever she was on dates, probably because she never went on them. But I really didn't know how to respond.

So I kissed him. Not just any kiss. I slobbed his chocolate ass down. I slowly let me hands glide across his big ass chest and abs, just to get a fill, and moved my waist closer to his, just to get a fill! Damn, he was fine.

"Okay, okay, goodnight Rakim..."

"Goodnight baby."

"Destiny is going to kill me," I thought to myself.

To Be Continued

PART 6

"Fraternal Fantasy"

-Tacara

I creeped inside, and the first thing I noticed was Briana passed out in Destiny's bed. I'm guessing they would've spent hours discussing the details of her date but I didn't have time for that shit. I went straight to the mirror to fix myself. I looked down at the outfit they'd put together and must say I was fairly impressed. I slightly teased my hair, added darker lipstick and eyeshadow and was on my way out the door.

I'd been familiar with some of the clubs around, but a club called "Taste," had to have been my favorite one. I got in Destiny's Camry and was on my way.

As soon as I pulled up, I noticed the banners and streamers placed on the doors and the light post. I figured it must be some type of celebration for the students. I was so wrong, and thank God I was. The party was being hosted by the Sigmas who had just had a line come out the same day. 8 brothers in that royal blue and pure white, I almost passed the hell out.

I made myself comfortable at the bar and ordered a Long Island Ice Tea, with sprite instead of coke. The party was being DJ'd by Kujho, so I couldn't help but slowly dance in my seat and sip at the same time. When the boys started to stroll, so did my eyes.

DJ Kujho played "Knuck if you buck" by Crime Mobb and the entire club got too crunk! Every sorority and fraternity in the building started to stroll. As they began hopping and strolling, I wasn't sure if I had pee'd on myself a little bit or came, and really didn't care.

After a few hours, I became tiresome. Which was never a good thing, because that meant Destiny would be coming back soon. I needed to find somebody to fuck me good, and quick. In honor of the new line of Sigmas, I decided to show love to the boys in blue.

I was headed out the door when I tall, slim brother grabbed my wrist and spun me around.

"Excuse me ma'am, where you headed?" He asked.

"Home, I am exhausted..." I replied, yawning and moving my wrist out of his hand.

"So soon? The party just started." He said while displaying his gorgeous smile.

I sized him up and down with my eyes seductively, and the brother was on point. He was about 6'3, slim athletic build, a low cut fade, soft brown skin, some perfect, pink lips and eyes that looked like he was mixed with Asian. He had on a blue PBS tank that showed off his perfect body and the eighteenth letter of the Greek alphabet branded firmly on his right shoulder.

I moaned softly to myself. "Damn..."

"Let me at least get you a drink? You look thirsty?" He said politely.

"Trust me, I am but it's not for a drink, so cut the crap. I just wanna fuck, just like you. No strings attached, no bullshit, and no commitments! So, what's your name? Where do you stay? And how many nuts you think I can get with you?" I replied with ease.

He looked around as if he was on a hidden camera show.

"Huh? Are you for real?" He asked with one eyebrow raised.

"Fuck it..." I said as I started to walk away.

He quickly followed behind me...
And began speaking fast!

"I'm Lee Brooks, I stay 3 minutes down the street and you can bust at least 6 nuts off of me, let's just say it's my magic number!" He responded, then smiled and turned around to show me the "6" on his back.

"Let's roll... I'll follow you..." I responded as he hurried to his car.

We walked into his place and it was surprisingly neat and tidy, things you wouldn't expect to see in a young bachelor pad. He opened the door to his room and immediately started to unbuckle his pants.

"Hold up!" I responded, "allow me."

I sat on the edge his bed and pulled him by his belt loops closer to me. I slowly unzipped his zipper and slid his shorts down right below his knees. He started to take his boots off...

"Leave them on." I requested. And he smiled.

He was wearing some baby blue American eagle briefs and his dick bulge made my pussy so wet. I pulled it out and began to suck it. I could taste his pre-cum immediately. He wanted it just as bad as I did. He locked his fingers, and placed both hands behind his head, while I served him with the best head of the year.

After a few minutes, he took his right hand and slid his fingers into my shorts, and made direct contact with my clit. I don't know what happened, but I felt my pants instantly get wet and my entire body tingled.

"One," I whispered lightly.

Then, he took his shirt off, so I did then same. He laid my flat on his bed, and kissed me literally from my forehead to my toes. Seductively rolling his tongue down my stomach and kissing my inner thigh. And kissed all around my clit before even touching it. I moaned and grabbed the back of his head.

"Two!" I shouted!

He then raised my legs up, to where my thighs were pressed against my stomach like he was changing my diaper, and ate the fuck out of me. Never, and I do mean never has a man made my body feel this way!

"Three!" I moaned aloud!

After that, he turned my body over and placed a pillow under my stomach...

"Now, lift it up so I can taste it from back here..." He demanded.

"Yes sir," I replied because he was punishing this pussy. I felt like I was in "Getting booty boot camp!"

I slowly raised my ass in the air and he laid on his back and slid under my body, like a mechanic working on a car.

"Fuck my face..." He exclaimed. As I motioned my body up and down on his tongue! I began groping and gyrating my body to the music that was playing from his phone. "Motivation" by Kelly Rowland. I could relate to every word she was singing.

"Ff-fa-ff four!" I yelled out as my pussy Juices flowed in his mouth! "I can't take no more!"

"Naw lil momma, I told you 6, so that's what you're going to get!" He replied as he slid from under me.

I laid there after he stopped eating me, body tingling, as he slowly stroked his big black dick inside of me from behind. He caressed my clit with the tip of his dick before sliding it in me. Slowly, then he began to speed up the pace.

I heard him make a sucking sound while he was hitting it from the back so I looked over my left shoulder to see what he was doing. He licked his fingers and then pulsated his fingertips on my clit!

I moaned so loud!

His motion was perfect! I felt like I was being fucked by Usher or Chris Brown because the motion of his hips felt like he was a dancer! It was the perfect choreography!

"FIVE!!!! Five!!!" I yelled and moaned loudly as he kept hitting it from the back!

"You want me to stop? Huh you want me to stop?" He asked me still going 100 MPH inside of me!

"Hell, we're almost to six!" I yelled back!

My entire body shook like a vibrator!

"I'm about to cum!"

"Me too!!!"

"Ahhhhhhhhhhh"

I could feel his aftershocks from nutting, and it felt so good. He laid his dick on the surface of my ass cheeks and laid his body on top of mine.

"Six." He whispered in my ear...

To Be Continued...

PART 7

"Fraternal Fantasy"

-Destiny

The morning after my date with Rakim, I was so hungover. I wasn't even really sure how things had ended on our date night. But I was quickly reminded by a text message from him:

"Last night was amazing! I can still feel your lips on mine. Ms. Destiny, I hope you have a great day & I can't wait for you to meet my brother today."

Kiss? I thought to myself! No! How in the hell could I have made out with him and didn't remember! Enough was enough, these blackouts were ruining my life. I had to call my mom.

"Morning baby, you're up early, how are you?" Mom asked hesitantly.

"I'm okay momma, yeah, I'm okay. How are you?"

"Destiny Marie, don't lie to me! What's wrong with you?" My mom snapped back. Whenever black parents add a middle name in their statement, it usually means, they mean business.

"It's nothing really momma, just sort of spaced out.. I'm losing track of time and events, I don't know what's going on honestly. But it's nothing to worry about..."

"How long has this been happening?" She asked.

"I'm not really sure, but for a while. I just never thought to pay much attention to it."

"Are you taking something?! I know you and Bri not smoking that mojo! Oh lord! Her mom is going to have a fit!"

"Momma, momma, chill! No ma'am, we're not smoking or doing any drugs outside of the occasional Biotin vitamins, I promise momma."

"Okay honey, well, why don't you go and talk to somebody, someone who can help both of us understand what's going on, I'll look up a few places around USM and I want you to go first thing in the morning, you hear?" One thing about my mom was she always made me feel safe.

"Yes ma'am..."

I hung up the phone with my mom and continued on with my day. I was about to meet my boyfriend's twin brother and it honestly made me nervous. To think someone as fine as Rakim, has a clone. Damn, that's just too much chocolate. I picked out a slightly conservative attire to meet for my lunch date with the guys. I didn't want his brother to think I was a thot.

I heard a knock at my room door...

"Come in..." I shouted aloud as if it would be someone besides Bri.

"Are you decent?" I heard a Rakim's voice say.

"Well, I thought I was before I started dating you." I responded as he peeked into my room and smiled.

"Oh really?" He asked with one eyebrow raised as he embraced me for what would be our second kiss.

His lips were so soft and big, they tasted like sweet mint and his tongue softly grazed mine. I felt my body tingle, my hands began to sweat and my heart began to race. All these things usually led to my blackouts, so I backed away! I slowly pushed his chest away from me to give me some space.

"I'm sorry, I just... Sorry." I began to fumble over my words because I felt lightheaded.

"Is everything okay?" Rakim asked as I stood there like a deer in headlights.

"I'm fine, I'm fine, just got a little lightheaded. Would you mind waiting in the living room while I finish?" I asked politely.

"Sure baby, no problem." He replied.

I stood in the mirror and gave myself a pep-talk. I wasn't sure what was happening with me but I wasn't going to let it get in the way of my new relationship.

We made small talk from my bedroom to the living room. Literally, making each other laugh with every statement. There was something so different about Rakim, almost like I knew him from another lifetime.

"So I think you should probably take it light on the drinking today Ms. Destiny." He said as we were leaving my apartment.

"I'm fine and grown, I can handle a beverage or 2."

"I know, I know, but last night something changed. It wasn't bad, but you seemed different." He replied.

"How so?" I asked.

"I'm not really sure, but I liked it. Whatever it was." He responded and I smiled.

What was happening to me? I asked myself.

We arrived at Chili's Bar & Grill and immediately we were greeted by 3 waitresses that seemed to have been quite smitten over Rakim. One thing I did find slightly intimidating was everyone's attraction to him. Every girl in or around campus loved him! He even had a couple of gay guys who hit on him repeatedly. But Rakim didn't feed into much of the attention, his eyes were always on me, literally.

"Destiny? Are you sure you're okay?" He asked snapping me out of my trance from the other side of the table.

"I'm fine, stop asking me that, I just need a drink." I replied attempting to play it off.

We ordered the triple dipple appetizer and 3 Presidente Margaritas. After about 20 minute of conversation, in walked the most gorgeous black man I've ever seen in my life.

Rakim lied. They were identical but so different. They shared the same lips, same nose, eyes, cheek bones, and smile. But Hakeem's body looked like he worked out for breakfast, lunch and twice for dinner. He's bald, with a beard that I would comb for him daily! His style was not southern. Most southern men would wear Levi's, a polo and loafers. Not Hakeem. He had on a tight fitted black sweater, some dark denim jeans, some black Kenneth Cole boots, which complimented his black ass all too well. These brothers were truly a gift from God.

"You must be Ms. Destiny?" He said while grabbing my right hand and placing a juicy kiss on my knuckles.

"Ugh, yes, Hakeem right?" I said as if my panties weren't literally soak and wet.

"Yes, Hakeem Abdul, I'm Rakim's better half." They shared a smile as Rakim got up from the booth to greet him with a hug.

"Better half hug?" Rakim asked jokingly.

"Yeah nigga you heard me now get up and hug a brother I just drove 4 hours to see your dusty black ass!"

They embraced one another, and it was magical. I could see their love for one another just from the way they looked at each other.

"I missed you Bubba."

"I missed you too."

Shit, I wanted to tell him I missed him too and had never seen him before! This was trouble!

To Be Continued...

PART 8

"Fraternal Fantasy"

-Destiny

As I sat there listening to them chat and adding my two cents every now and then. I noticed how the bond I felt with Rakim, was immediately the same with Hakeem. It was easy to talk to them, and the respect they have for everyone amazed me. "I hope I marry this man.." I thought to myself. After lunch we headed over to Rakim's place to talk and have a couple more drinks. This could either be a good thing or a bad thing, we'll see.

We made ourselves comfortable on the sofa, and Rakim turned on the game and handed us some cold beers out of the fridge.

"I'm going to take a shower," Rakim announced. "You two get to know each other better, I'll be right back."

The thought of Rakim taking off all of his clothes sent chills up my spine. I needed to calm down I could feel myself fading away, literally, from the thought.

-Tacara

See, here's the thing. I'm not with that gushy, fairytale shit. See, Destiny is sitting here thinking, "oh my gosh, they're perfect, Hakeem's going to be the perfect uncle." And I'm here thinking, "when and where can I fulfill my fantasy of fucking twins!" It was time for me to show my face.

"So Hakeem, you work out a lot I'm guessing?" I asked while Rakim was taking a shower.

"Ha, yeah actually I do, about 4 times a week. Can you tell?" He asked smiling from ear to ear and raising his shirt to show off his abs. He really didn't have to lift his shirt because I could see his physique through his tight ass black sweater.

"Oh my damn.." The words slipped out of my mouth before I knew it. "Yes, I can tell, do you train?"

"That's actually what I do, I'm a fitness coach in Oxford, Mississippi." He said with a hard southern slang. "I make a pretty decent living for myself and it makes me feel good. It's like a project. I can take someone who doesn't feel so confident about themselves, and mold them to exactly what they wanted to be or look like."

He could mold me any day.

"Soo let's say I wanted to be trained. Could you assist me with that?" I asked as he looked over his left shoulder to see if his brother was still in the bathroom.

"Yeah, I maybe could do that? What areas are you trying to work on?" He asked. "It helps if I can see them."

I stood up to give him a more detailed view.

I lifted my shirt showing off my flat stomach.

"Maybe get me some abs..." I said while moving my hand up and down my stomach, and slowly lowering my pantie line to show off a little more.

Then I turned around and cuffed my ass checks,

"Maybe lift my ass a little." I said and he nodded as I jiggled my ass.

"Is there something we could do with these?" I asked while cupping both my breast, pushing them close together.

"Ummm yeah, I'm sure there's a few things I could think of.." He said nervously, constantly turning around to see if his brother was coming.

He took his right hand and readjusted his dick, I guess to make it point downward, and not stand straight up.

"Ms. Destiny I think you should definitely sign up for a couple of my classes."

"I'm all in." I winked and started walking closer to him.

"Okay, okay!" He said nervously but I didn't care, but then...

"All in for what?" Rakim came around the corner exposing all of his 8 pack, with a white towel wrapped around his waist.

"Damn." I said to myself.

I looked down at my hands and felt them begin to tingle. Never has this happened to me before. I wasn't sure what was coming over me, but I felt sick to my stomach. I think Destiny was coming back. What the fuck!

-Destiny

I looked around the room at both brothers and couldn't fathom to admit that I had lost track of the last few minutes. I stood there looking lost with my shirt elevated in the middle of the living room and Rakim was standing there fresh out of the shower.

I smiled gracefully and decided my mom was right. I needed to see someone about this.

"Destiny you okay baby?" Rakim asked looking at me with one eyebrow raised.

"I'm fine, I just need to go home and lie down.." I responded.

"Alright, let me put on some clothes and I'll take you.." Rakim responded, and Hakeem was looking at me like I was crazy.

What was happening to me?

To be continued...

PART 9

"Fraternal Fantasy"

I told my mom everything that happened and she finally took it upon herself to book me an appointment. She hated the fact that she wasn't close enough to come every time I called, but she was confident that a doctor was exactly what I needed.

The next morning I had a doctor's appointment with Dr. Drew, not knowing this would be the doctor that would change my life.

I sat nervously in the waiting room trying to figure out exactly what I was going to tell her. I had taken enough psychology classes to know what to say and what not to say, but honestly I did feel like I was borderline, losing my damn mind.

All that I could gather about myself is that I was losing track of time, nothing else really made any sense.

"Dr. Drew will see you now." I tall, slender, blonde haired white girl came to tell me.

I stood up and walked into her office, which was clean, tidy and organized perfectly. It actually soothed my anxiety.

Dr. Drew was amazingly beautiful. Not exactly what I pictured when I booked the appointment with a psych doctor. She was a slim built black woman, with soft mocha skin, perfect teeth, a shoulder-length bob haircut, black eyeglass frames, perfectly arched eyebrows and dressed similar to me. She was gorgeous.

"Hi Dr. Drew," I said as we greeted each other with a handshake.

"Hi Destiny, how are you?" She asked, and I felt like I was being diagnosed right away.

"I'm okay... I just... Never mind." I felt that the first thing I wanted to do was to cry aloud and tell her everything that was going on immediately but I didn't want her to think I was crazy. Not so soon, anyway.

"Well Destiny, I understand you're interest in psychology from your transcript but I want you to remove all feelings that you have towards lectures and studies you've learned in your Psychology courses. I want you to be opened minded. And understand that any and every thing we discuss from here on out is strictly between you and myself. So I'll ask again, how are you?"

"Honestly, I'm lost. *I took a deep breath* I'm losing track of time, that's why I came to see you today." I responded.

"And How long has this been happening? The losing track of time?" She asked.

"I'm not really sure," I rubbed my left hand through my hair to express my frustration.

"It's been happening for quite some time but I'm just realizing it now." I responded.

"Tell me, what does it feel like when you wake up or come to after losing track of time." She said while making herself comfortable and sitting down beside me. "Is it okay if I record us?"

"That's fine. But it started off happening at night time. I would go to sleep and then wake up, look in the mirror, and sometimes I could barely recognize myself."

"What do you mean, explain."

"Well like, the other night I went on a date with my boyfriend, Rakim. It was a simple dinner, and conversation.. But..."

"Did you drink?" She asked while taking notes.

"No, I mean yes ma'am, but not enough to have a black out I promise you." I responded defensively.

"I'm just asking, but continue."

"We shared an amazing night of talking and getting to know each other even better. I was talking about my family, and he even told me about his. As the night came to an end, so does my memory of the night. Then, the next morning I woke up and he told me we shared our first kiss. Can I tell you something Dr. Drew?" I asked with tears in my eyes.

"Go ahead Destiny." She said, moving closer to me.

"I'm still a virgin, but my body doesn't feel like I am." Tears began falling from my face. "I've never even had an orgasm that I could remember but I have vivid dreams of me having sex all the time. Like so vivid that I can remember how the person felt, or smelled. And sometimes when I see these people in person, it's almost like they have the dreams of me. Like we've actually had sex. I know, I sound crazy but..."

Dr. Drew sat back some to get a better look at me. She grabbed a pink box of Kleenex off of her desk and handed it to me.

"We're going to figure this out Destiny, don't cry." I looked up at Dr. Drew and I could feel the reassurance in her time of voice. I was confident that she would change everything for me. We spent about an hour discussing different strategies that would help me in my journey to make myself better.

That night as I drove home I thought about some of the methods Dr. Drew had discussed with me to help find the trigger for my black outs. She asked me to refrain from alcohol, birth control and even my biotin supplements until I figured out exactly what was triggering my loss of time.

"Roommate! Where have you been?" Bri came running to me as if someone had just died! I'd turned my phone off just for a little while to help gather my thoughts.

"Bri, calm down, I had a doctor's appointment, is everything okay?" I responded with urgency.

"Hakeem came by, Rakim was in an accident, let's go!" Bri grabbed her keys off the counter, grabbed my right hand and we rushed to her car!

My heart began racing and pounding out of my chest! Why did I feel so much pain and care for a man I had just met. The thought of losing him devastated me. I had hospitals and tragedy.

I closed my eyes and said a prayer.

I had a flashback

September 11, 1997

"Mom what happened? Where's dad?!" I asked crying from the backseat.

"Everything's going to be fine, calm down Dee." My brother Devin said trying to ease my mind.

"where are we going?" I cried aloud, not understanding what had just happened!

"Things are going to change from here on out Destiny. Your dad was shot and killed." My mom said glancing at

*me in the rear-view mirror with blood on her sleeves.
"Things are going to change."*

"We're here Destiny! Come on!" Bri said, snapping me
out of my daydream.

To be continued.

PART 10

"Fraternal Fantasy"

-Destiny

As I walked down the halls of the hospital, I felt
myself become extremely anxious and nervous. I didn't
know what to expect. Hakeem had given Bri very little
information on the accident so we came as soon as
possible. So many questions ran through my mind. Like,
why did Hakeem feel the need to come tell us about the
accident? I felt flattered considering the fact that we'd
only been dating for such a short period of time.

As soon as we turned the corner there were 3 older
women and Hakeem sitting outside his room.

"Hey Hakeem, is he doing okay?" I asked, feeling
slightly out of place. I mean, we'd only been dating for a
short period of time but I felt so close to him.

"He's fine..." Hakeem embraced me with a tight, heartfelt
hug, and then gave one to Bri as well. "Thanks for
coming D, he asked about you numerous times.

I smiled.

The older lady in the middle stood up, and I took a couple steps towards her.

"Hi, I'm..."

"Destiny... I recognize you anywhere, my son hasn't stopped talking about you since he met you in the science lab. It's so nice to finally meet you." His mom exclaimed and I felt my cheeks blushing. The thought of Rakim mentioning me outside of my presence felt flattering.

"Really, it's a pleasure to meet you Mrs. Abdul, it's an honor to meet the woman who raised such gentleman as Rakim and Hakeem are." I responded as she kissed me on my left cheek.

"Thank you baby..." She said softly. "Now go ahead and talk to Rakim, let him know we'll be here to see him in the morning."

"Yes ma'am, and Bri, I'll go ahead and stay here for a while, go ahead and go home, I know you have an exam to study for."

I walked in to see Rakim and my heart dropped. He was tied up to all different machines, and he had a huge cast over his right arm and collar bone. I softly kissed his cheek trying not to wake him.

"Hey baby..." He whispered, slowly opening his eyes, and flashing his flawless smile.

"Hey baby, are you feeling okay?" I asked trying to whisper as if speaking loudly would hurt him. I grazed his hair with my fingertips slowly.

"I'm fine baby, I'm fine. I should've been wearing my seatbelt, that's all. I missed you today, how'd it go at your appointment." He asked as if I were the one who was injured.

"We'll discuss that later baby..." I responded.

"Thanks for coming baby, did you meet my mom?" He asked with excitement.

"I did, I think she likes me." I said confidently.

"I'm sure she does."

"Well, I know we haven't spent a night with each other, but I was wondering if you would mind staying with me tonight." He asked and it made my heart melt.

"Of course baby, I was going to ask you the same thing." I responded. "I already told Bri she could leave me here."

"Thanks baby," he said grabbing my hand.

I slid the visitor bench up to his bed, and laid my head on his bed. We talked until he fell fast asleep. "This man was so amazing..." I thought to myself.

Around 3am I woke up from the sounds of my iPhone. It had 5 missed text messages from Bri.

I checked them, responded, then positioned myself on the couch to go back to sleep. I looked up at Rakim laying comfortably on the bed, and got up to kiss his lips softly. Even all strapped down on the hospital bed, he was gorgeous. After I felt my lips leave from his I couldn't help but look down at his dick print and I was instantly turned on. There was something about a man's dick print that drove me insane. Everything in me told me to just go lie down on the couch, but another part of me just wanted to touch it.

Just once.

Just touch it, that's all.

I listened to his breathing pattern and softly grazed my hand across the head of his dick print. He moaned softly and I immediately took my hand away. When I sat down I noticed that I must have started something because I could see it moving up and down under the covers. I instantly got wet. Damn!

-Tacara

After listening to her whine to the doctor about me today, I seriously tried not to show my face again. But I couldn't help it. Let's just say, I'm here to protect her.

After she got all steamed up from her little touch and go with Rakim's dick, I got up to go please her, big time.

I walked out of the hospital room quietly and the first thing I noticed was the nurses' station. There was nothing sexier than a man in scrubs but a doctor would be better. I walked up and down the hallways like a bitch in heat but there was nothing. So I decided to just simply go lie back down with Rakim, and let Destiny enjoy waking up to her sex-less, boring ass relationship with his cripple ass.

As I walked up to Rakim's room, out walked a cute, slim built, light skin brother. Not really my taste, but he could probably get it. He had on some sky blue scrubs, with glasses and a notepad.

"Umm hi," he said nervously, almost bumping into me.

"Hi nurse," I waved trying to be cute.

He took a step left to move out of my way, but I just took a step right with him.

"Ummm nurse, do you know where I could get a snack around here? The vending machine was out of order..." I said while standing just a couple inches from his face.

He took a deep breath, I could tell he was nervous. He pushed his glasses closer to his face.

"Umm you umm could maybe try the umm vending machine on the pediatric floor, number 2..." He said trying to ease his way from in front of me.

"Thanks Nurse, did you want something to? I would feel so bad getting myself a treat and not offering you something in return. I have more than just snacks to offer." I was a thot straight off the dome.

"No ma'am, I better get back to work, excuse me." He said eagerly.

"Wait..." I paused him by seductively caressing his stomach with my right hand.

"Are you sure there's nothing I could do for you?" I eased my hand lower towards his dick just to rub on it.

"Isn't that your boyfriend in there?" He asked.

"Nope, that's my sister's man. Come on."

"Wait!" He whispered, but I was too persistent.

I eased Rakim's room door open, went into the bathroom and turned on the shower to drain out any noise.

"I don't know about this, I could get in a lot of trouble." He responded.

"We're good, now drop them." I said motioning my hands for him to drop his scrubs.

As he slowly unfastened the strings in his scrubs I could see that this nerdy looking light skin boy wasn't going to be so lame in the sheets. The shaft of his dick looked about 9 inches. I had to taste it. It stood straight up from the whole in his boxers, which coincidentally matched his scrubs.

I got on my knees and began to give him head. He was very calm and modest so I took his right hand and placed it on the back of my neck, then took his left hand and put it on my breast. He was definitely an amateur, I could tell from his quickness to precum.

He began to thrust in my mouth and I could taste the precum getting stronger, as if he was to the point of ejaculation. He moaned softly.

"Slow down..." I whispered.

"I can't!" He whispered loudly, speeding up the motions of his hips.

He was almost there when we heard a knock at the bathroom door.

"Destiny, you okay in there?" Rakim said from the other side of the door.

I looked up at the nurse with his penis still in my mouth.

"FUCKKK" I read his lips say.

To be continued...

PART 11

"Fraternal Fantasy"

-Destiny

I'm not exactly sure why but when I woke up I was in the shower with the water pouring all over my hair and face. The last thing I could remember was lying next to Rakim's hospital bed, then I somehow ended up in here. I heard some commotion going on outside the shower curtain, so I slowly peeled it back.

"Rakim WHAT ARE YOU DOING?! PUT HIM DOWN!!" I screamed, attempting to cover my breast with the shower curtain, and reaching for a towel!

"You're not even supposed to be out of the bed!" I exclaimed as Rakim held some male nurse by his neck, in the bathroom! What the hell was going on?!

"You fucking this nigga Destiny, don't lie to me!" Rakim yelled with anger in his eyes!

"Fucking him? Rakim what? What's wrong with you! He's your nurse, I was in the shower! Stop it!" I held my towel over my wet body, and used my right arm to force Rakim to let the man breathe.

"Then why the fuck is he is the bathroom with you and his little fucking dick was on hard and shit! Huh can one of you explain that?!" Rakim was so mad, and hurt. This was the first time I'd ever heard him say any curse words. He stood there with his hand around his neck, waiting for one of us to respond.

"I-I-I-came into...." The nurse began to explain but something came over me. It was almost like I was covering up a lie for someone else.

"Earlier when he came to check your signs, I asked him to bring some towels and soap baby, I'm guessing that's what he was doing? Why he was in the bathroom while I was in the shower, I don't know.. But you know I wouldn't cheat on you. Stop!" I responded and I could see Rakim calming down, and the nurse sense of relief. I wasn't even sure if I was telling the truth or not, I couldn't remember a thing.

"So you were just here to bring towels?" Rakim asked him with his hand still tight around the collar of the nurse's scrubs. "Huh? Answer me?!"

"That's it Mr. Rakim, big brother sir!" The nurse saluted him and I looked at him funny.

"Big brother?" I whispered quietly to myself.

"Get out and I'll see you tomorrow night!" He exclaimed to the nurse as he power walked out of the room.

I wanted to know what the big brother comment was all about, but figured this was no time to ask.

Rakim took a deep breath and then turned to me with remorse in his eyes.

"Baby I'm sorry, I just didn't know what was going on. I didn't know if he was trying to peak at you or fuck you or what. I'm sorry Destiny."

"I'm just going to go Rakim, would you mind getting out so I can finish drying off?" I exclaimed as Rakim came to hug me, I pushed him away. "Now! Rakim!"

"Please don't leave me baby, I'm sorry. Please."

He walked out of the bathroom with half of a hospital rob on exposing his entire back side, and his head hung how.

When he closed the door, I looked in the mirror and tears began streaming from my face. Something was wrong. I didn't know that male nurse, but my body sure as hell did. Something had went wrong, I just didn't know what.

It was time to talk to Dr. Drew again.

To be continued...

PART 12

"Fraternal Fantasy"

-Destiny

That night I went ahead and spent the night with Rakim, but just until he fell back asleep. He was so high off the medication, I wouldn't be surprised if he didn't remembered anything from the night before, like almost killing an RN. It had gotten completely out of control, and I felt I was the blame. I didn't know why I felt like it was my fault, but I did.

The next morning I called my mom to make an emergency meeting for myself and Dr. Drew. My mom asked a series of questions and decided she needed to plan an emergency trip to come see me. I mean, what was really going on with me?

I made it to Dr. Drew's office around 10AM, she was the only person in the building and had made herself completely available for me. I guess she could sense the urgency from my mom's voice.

"Good morning Destiny, I got you some donuts and coffee. How you feeling today?" Dr. Drew asked handing me the box of Krispy Kreme.

"No thanks Doctor, I have no appetite. Things have gotten worse." I explained and I felt my eyes watering.

"How so? What's new? I'm listening." She asked.

"Last night I stayed with my boyfriend Rakim in the hospital. He was in an accident, but he's doing okay now, they just kept him for observational purposes. Everything was going fine, but I somehow ended up in the shower, with a male nurse half naked in the bathroom with me. Rakim almost killed him. But I swear to you I didn't know that nurse but I sensed it was my fault he was in that bathroom last night. Like I can't explain, but I seriously felt like it was me that lured him into the bathroom last night."

"Wait, calm down Destiny? How'd you end up in the shower? Can you remember what triggered the black out this time?" Dr. Drew asked sincerely.

"No ma'am, I just..." I paused. Remembering my little touch and go with Rakim's penis.

"You just what? What's the last thing you remember?" She asked.

I looked up at her nervously.

"I'm not really sure, but I..."

"Don't be afraid to talk to me, it's the only way to figure this thing out Destiny."

"Well my boyfriend was lying on the bed, flat on his back! Don't think I'm a pervert! Please! But I just wanted to touch it, that's all just touch it once." I responded nervously. "As he laid there I could see his dick bulging from the sheets. I just wanted to grab it one time."

"It's normal for you to feel a strong sexual attraction to him, don't be ashamed. Did you touch it? And how did I make you feel?" She asked.

"Yes, I caressed it and I heard his body moan and it made me so wet.." I explained and I could feel my body start to tingle and my panties got wet from the thought of it. This was never a good thing, but I think we were about to see my black outs first hand.

"And then what happened Destiny? Destiny?" Are you okay?" Dr. Drew shook me.

-Tacara

I took off Destiny's hideous Ray Banns.

"Doctor, what happened next is I stepped in." I responded with a smile.

"You stepped in? Who are you?" She adjusted herself in the seat and make sure her recorder was working.

"I'm Tacara. I'm Destiny's other half or should I say better half." I responded.

"So you two share the same body? Or what exactly do you share?" Dr. Drew asked.

"Everything, except sex. I won't allow her to have it. It's just that simple. That's why she think she's a virgin, because she's barely ever seen a real penis. I'm her protector." I exclaimed.

"How long have you been around?" She asked.

"Since I died, years ago, and was embraced by the soul of Destiny. I've protected her ever since.

"You died? How? And why'd you chose Destiny?" Dr. Drew asked.

"It's complicated, but I was killed. But... Never mind. Maybe Destiny can tell you the story someday." I responded.

"If you wouldn't mind, I'd like to try a simple test with you, if that's okay?" Dr. Drew asked.

"Whatever..."

We stepped over to a white line tapped across the floor.

"Stand here, can you read those letters for me?" Dr. Drew asked.

"Yea sure, E, F, T, L, P, E, D, P, C, T, F, H, D," I recited her entire sight chart from largest to smallest, top to bottom.

"That's weird, Destiny could barely read the second line without her glasses..." Dr. Drew added.

"Okay, that's interesting. So Tacara tell me, how do I get Destiny back?" She asked.

"I don't know, but I only come when she gets turned on. Try singing gospel or something." I said and then chuckled.

"Amazing grace how sweet the sound that saved a wretch like me!" Dr. Drew was really singing and I was cracking up.

"I was joking doctor! It won't work!" She continued.

"I once was lost but now I'm found, was blind but now I see...."

-Destiny

"Dr. Drew you have a gorgeous voice, but why are you singing to me?" I asked.

To be continued...

PART 13

"Fraternal Fantasy"

-Destiny

"It's a long story, but we'll get into later, okay?" Dr. Drew asked. "Listen Destiny, this is slightly more serious than I expected but don't panic, we'll figure it out I promise."

"But why were you singing, is it a trigger?" I asked.

"Something like that... I'm going to schedule an appointment to talk to your mom about your childhood that you're having trouble remembering." Dr. Drew responded.

I left her office more confused than I started, but I had to go check on Rakim, who had just been released from the hospital. I stopped at Walmart to grab a couple items we'd need for our Science lab coming up and even a couple items to make him a great dinner.

I listening to the gospel song: Donald Lawrence: "Encourage yourself." To get my mind right before heading to Rakim's. I picked up all the items for a salad and purchase a couple things to make some pasta. And I'm not going to lie, I was extremely horny, but Dr. Drew advised me to stay away from porn, touching myself, or anything that remotely reminded me of sex.

I knocked on Rakim's door and there was a note with my name attached to his apartment door:

"Dear Ms. Destiny, the last few days have been crazy but thank you for being there for me in more ways than one. When you come inside, I've done everything to show my apology. P.S. I think I'm falling in love with you..."

My heart melted. Here I was planning the perfect night for him, and he had the same idea. Truth is, I was falling in love with him to. But I would eventually have to tell him about the black outs.

I walked in and there were rose pedals, t-light candles, the smell of a delicious meal cooking, the smell of vanilla candles, and there he was, half-crippled laying on the couch with his shirt off and a sling on his arm. He immediately got up to give me a kiss that made my knees so weak. I softly pushed him away.

"Baby what's all this?" I asked.

"It's for you. It's all for you baby. I know it's only been a few months, but Destiny you are the one. I'm not asking for your hand in marriage but I am asking to be exclusive with you. No one has ever made me feel the way you have. And my momma! She can't stop talking about how beautiful you are and how dumb I would be to let you go. I need you baby. Let's sit down." Rakim announced. And my heart began pounding.

He pulled out my seat and he had prepared the most extravagant meal I'd ever seen.

"You know I'm a southern gentleman, so I prepared you a meal just like momma used to make it."

It made steak, baked potatoes, yams, a salad, and some red wine on the side. My mouth began to water.

He sat down at the other end of the table and we began to converse and eat the delicious meal he'd prepared.

"How is it baby?" He asked.

"It's just as amazing as you are Rakim." I could see him smile and blush.

"What's all that you brought?" He asked pointing at the bags I brought.

"Well since you weren't supposed to be moving, I was going to make you dinner and finish our project for tomorrow's class, graduation is just a few days away.." I replied.

He pointed to the left.

"I already finished it Baby." Pointing at the immaculate sculpture he had done himself with one arm.

"I love you Rakim,"

"I love you too Destiny..."

After a delicious dinner and a movie, we got comfortable and settled off to sleep. This was going to be our first night sleeping side by side in the same bed. I was nervous because of what Dr. Drew said but I was determined to suppress my urges.

We took showers separately but when he got out, I almost fainted. His body looked like a Greek-God!

"Baby can you help me?" He asked pointing to the cream on the side of his bed that his doctor instructed him to put on his wounds.

"Sure baby, and here's your medicine." I rubbed his arms and I felt my body going crazy. But I was maintaining my innocence by not thinking about how sexy he looked and felt.

We laid next to each other on the bed, and I felt him spoon me. I could feel his dick in the crack of my ass.

"Damn!" I whispered as I heard him snoring! This isn't good, but at least we'll both be sleep when I black out!

To be continued...

PART 14

"Fraternal Fantasy"

-Tacara

I Yawned

I felt both of them fall fast asleep and I couldn't help but go please myself. I was going to just go to the bathroom and play with myself but fuck that. I needed some D. I needed to cum!

I slid my left hand down my back and felt Rakim's hard dick on Destiny's ass, I simply stroked it, got myself wet. And slid out of the bed. I may have been a hoe, but I wouldn't come between her and Rakim.

I was wearing nothing but pajamas but since he stayed in some college apartments as well, I knew it wouldn't hurt to go out on the prowl for just a second.

I quietly walked out of his room and apartment and there was a gang of dudes sitting outside smoking weed and talking shit. I really wanted to be a good girl but there was one guy standing tall and sexy and dark as hell. I needed him. Just a taste! That's all!

"Can I hit that?" I asked reaching for the blunt they were passing around.

"Hey yeah lil momma!" They said collectively, checking out my ass and bra-less breast.

"I'm Trey," the tall, sexy dark skinned one said with the prettiest smile, tattoos, and dressed like he had just left the gym.

"Tacara..." I replied.

"Damn T. It's kind of late for your sexy ass to be out alone huh?" Trey asked.

"I can take care of myself... Plus my sister is inside getting some, so I felt left out." I replied.

"Oh for real..." He replied grabbing his dick through his basketball shorts, with gloves on his hands like he had just finished lifting weights.

"You work out?" I asked seductively.

"Can't you tell?" He replied bouncing his pecs and my pussy started throbbing.

"Could you lift me?"

"Hell yeah, I could lift you flip you taste you dip you whatever lil momma."

"Oh really?" I asked.

"Want to find out?" He asked and I could see his dick print moving as he grabbed my hand and moved it towards it to touch it.

"Can I suck it here?"

"Wait, we outside though!" He said shockingly!

"You scared?" I asked.

"Hell naw! Let's walk away from them!" He said while pulling down his black basketball shorts, exposing his huge bulge.

He pulled it out and I immediately went to work, right outside of the apartments. He threw his head back and began to moan loudly. "Damn girl. You gon make me cream all down your throat!"

"Let's try something." He said.

He then grabbed my thighs and placed me on his shoulders with my pussy right on his lips! He pinned me up against the wall until I came over and over, then kissed me so I could taste myself! I looked down and could see his dick still rock hard!

I couldn't stop coming!

He then turned me upside down and made me do a hand-stand to where his dick was in my mouth and he was eating my ass like groceries! Still grasping my thighs so that my hands weren't even touching the sidewalk!

"Baby I'm about to bust! Can I nut in your mouth?!" He asked!

"Mmmhmmm" I mumbled as I felt his load go down my throat! I choked because it was so much! It tasted so good like vanilla!

He let me down, pulled up his pants as I wiped the remainder of his cum off of my cheeks.

"Your nut taste so good!" I exclaimed.

"They don't call me Frost HD for nothing!"

"This never happened, okay?" I demanded.

"Shit, cool with me."
He responded.

To be continued!

PART 15

"Fraternal Fantasy"

-Destiny (8 Months Later)

It's been a few months and I must say, I think things have gotten a lot better. Rakim and I decided to move in together, and to my knowledge, I haven't had any black-outs that I could remember. I think it had a lot to do with being around Rakim more, and trying my best to suppress any sexual urges. I must say, it's not easy being a 24 year old virgin. But somehow, my body felt like it didn't need it.

After graduation, Rakim and I both got great jobs working at a local high-school. He was coaching and teaching health, and I had become the 11th grade English teacher. Life couldn't get much better than this. So I thought.

Rakim was simply perfect. My mom loved everything about him, and so did my twin brothers Deshaun and Devin. My mom often came to visit us, and was anxious to have grand kids, but I didn't think we were ready for marriage, sex, and definitely not kids, just yet. I wanted to be a virtuous woman forever!

It was a Friday afternoon and Rakim had prepared a scrumptious dinner for our entire family. Both my brothers, his brother Hakeem, and my mother.

Of course there was no pork, but plenty of smothered chicken, fried chicken, scalloped potatoes, candied yams, collard greens and corn bread, with an exquisite bottle of Champaign. He always tried his best to impress my brothers and mother.

"Rakim, baby you have truly outdone yourself tonight! I can tell you have that southern green thumb because every meal you make is delicious!" My mom announced from the head of the table.

"Thanks Ms. Johnson, he learned it all from me." Hakeem said jokingly showing off his beautiful smile.

My mom and I were truly in heaven, around 2 sets of twins that were very respectable and had created quite the friendship.

"So can I ask a personal question?" My brother Devin asked aloud and I got nervous. He had recently came out the closet, as a gay man, so let's just say he had no filter when it came to the things he said.

"Devin!" My brother Deshaun kicked him under the table.

"Go ahead bro." Rakim responded.

"Well, I'm just wondering.. When do y'all plan on making it official? Cause I know you ain't tapping that ahh---" Deshaun kicked him again.

"Bruh, don't disrespect my mom like that, watch your mouth!" Deshaun cut him off.

"Well, honestly we were all thinking it!" My mom chuckled, while poking at the rest of the potatoes on her plate.

I smiled.

"Soon, soon..." Rakim replied while blushing.

After a great meal and dessert with my family, we continued to talk and laugh with one another.

"So Ms. Johnson, Destiny keeps it very limited when talking about Mr. Johnson, why is that?" Rakim asked nervously and I could tell my mom and brothers became anxious, looking at each other and wondering who would answer it first.

"Well, he was a good man. And Destiny probably doesn't mention him, because she vaguely remembers him. She was young when he passed away." My mom responded.

"But I thought she was 10, that's about how old I was when my dad passed away and I remember a lot about him... Not to pry, just wondering." Rakim replied and I could feel the tension at the table. "What happened to him, if you don't mind me asking?"

My mom took a sip of her drink and I could tell she was nervous about the answer. Truth was I remembered very little about him, and it was almost like a dream whenever I thought of him.

"He was in an accident," Deshaun answered.

"I'm sorry to hear that. I'm sure he was an amazing man."
Hakeem responded while smiling at my mom.

"Mmmph." My mom replied.

After a couple more drinks, Rakim had lit a few candles
on our balcony and made everyone comfortable outside.
He handed everyone a glass to pour Champaign. My
brother Devin was passed drunk and starting to irritate
my mom.

"Can I say something?" Rakim asked while we all sat
around in a circle still talking and telling memories of
our childhood.

"We're listening..." Hakeem replied to Rakim.

"Well as y'all know it's been a year since I met Ms.
Destiny in Dr. Wilson's lab class and ever since that day
my life has been somewhat of a fairy tale. I know I'm not
easy to deal with sometimes but I couldn't imagine a day
without you in my life. And that goes to Devin and
Deshaun too, we're like quadruplets now. I invited all of
you here today because I have a question for all 4 of
you." Rakim said, kneeling on one knee in front of me,
and my family with a ring bigger than I know he could
afford! My eyes got huge! My heart started racing and
my hands starting shaking!

"Oh my lord!" My mom exclaimed with excitement!

"When you marry someone, you don't just marry them,
but their entire family. So tonight, I ask you, Destiny,
Ms. Johnson, Devin, and Deshaun. Will you marry me?
And will you all allow me and Hakeem to be a part of
your family?" Tears began pouring from my eyes! I
could hear my mom sniffling, holding back tears.

"YESSS! Hell yes!" Devin screamed! And Deshaun punched him in his arm!

"Bruh chill out!" Deshaun said, I could tell he had become slightly choked up. Even though he always portrayed to act hard.

"Yes baby, I would be so blessed to spend the rest of my life with you." I replied and my mom started crying.

It was a beautiful night. I was now engaged!

To be continued.

PART 16

"Fraternal Fantasy"

-Destiny

It'd been a couple days since the proposal and everything was going GREAT! My fiancé, Rakim, was bragging to all the teachers we worked with, most of his buddies from the gym and my mom had literally told the entire world. My brother Devin told so many people, you would've thought he was the one getting married! When I posted our ring on Facebook it got over 400 likes! I felt so liberated to be marrying such an outstanding man. And he felt so blessed to be marrying someone as pure as myself. Just think, in a few months I would know how it felt to have a man I side of me. Kissing and touching had become mundane to Rakim and I, our bodies needed each other. He'd mentioned that he jacked off so much, he would switch up hands just to get a different feeling.

It was that following Monday when Bri and I had started planning some of the options for the wedding. She was more excited than I was, and of course she'd be my maid of honor, and I know it's nontraditional but I really wanted my brother, Devin, to be one of my brides-man, it just seemed right. He'd been one of my best friends my entire life. Not to mention, the colors of our wedding would be Crimson & Crème, expressing the tones of both his and Devin's fraternity and my sorority! Ooooo-op!

Deshaun and I were just as close as well but he's portrayed the role of my father, since we lost him at such a young age. Not to mention he and Hakeem got along so well because they were both dogs, I mean Omegas!

The day was progressing well, when Rakim came home upset and slamming things all around the house. I'd prepared a nice pot of seafood gumbo, which usually always put a smile on his face, just from the smell but today was different.

"Baby, what's your dang-on problem sir?" I asked jokingly to put a smile on his face.

He tried to hold back his smile but couldn't when it came to me. I had that power of making him smile even when he was furious!

"That damn Hakeem, I just don't know what to do about him!" He exclaimed with a look of frustration and his hand on his head! "I've prayed over and over that he finds his way but it's not getting any better and it's stressing me out!"

"Wait, calm down! What happened?" I asked.

"He lost his fitness training job, has been behind on his rent for 3 months, car note overdue, and just went to jail for some domestic dispute! It's literally killing my mom, it seems like he has no sympathy for her illness! I've had it up to here with his black ass Destiny! Can you hand me a beer baby? Please." He exclaimed while forcefully sitting on the couch with his hand on his forehead!

"Baby, calm down, it's going to be okay, I promise. Hakeem is a smart man, he'll figure something out." I responded while handing him a cold Bud Light.

"I know but when he's hurting, I'm hurting. I'm only as good as my brother, if that makes sense." He replied.

"Yes baby, my brothers go through the same thing. Being twins intensifies the brotherly love, I know baby. So what can we do to help, besides praying? Wait! I have an idea!" I responded.

"I'm listening baby." He said looking up at me still frustrated.

"Why doesn't he just move in with us? We have more than enough space. We can help him get a job at the school or from someone we know, and that way y'all can be together more. Because obviously he can't keep his head on straight without his bubba..." I explained and Rakim had the biggest smile on his face.

"Baby are you sure? That's another man living under your roof. Are you sure that'd be okay?" He asked looking in my eyes for reassurance.

"Baby, I'm positive. Anything to make you happy and less stressed. I'll call him today and tell him I have the guest room set up for him. And last time I talked to Deshaun he was in Jackson, so maybe he could help him get started tonight. No need in him getting into any more drama up there by himself, you know?" I replied kissing him on the forehead.

"Damn Destiny, how did I get so lucky?" He asked, and we kissed and smiled.

I'm guessing things were pretty bad with Hakeem because around 8 o'clock he and my brother Deshaun pulled up in his car and a U-Haul truck. I didn't think he'd be here so soon but I didn't mind at all.

I made them some fresh lemonade, while they proceeded to finish moving in all of Hakeem's things into our guest bedroom. I'd actually admired the fact that the 4 of them had become so close. Sometimes I felt left out, being the only one not a twin. But also, so protected having 4 brothers around me so much.

"Oh my damn!" Devin exclaimed as he watched Hakeem moving some of his things to his new room shirtless!

I hit him in his side!

"Ouch!"

"Don't be nasty, that's like practically hitting on my fiancé jerk, they look just alike!" I responded!

"Well Rakim Muslim ass could get it too!" He replied and we both chuckled!

"Shut up and let's help him finish."

"Wait though, have y'all discussed the issue of having a Muslim or Christian wedding? How is that going to work?" Devin's nosey ass asked.

"It's actually pretty cool, I have an awesome idea. Me, you and Bri will talk about it later, now being your lazy butt on." I replied grabbing his right hand and lifting him off the couch.

We got Hakeem all settled in and the night was coming to an end. Rakim had tired himself out from moving, and was passed out in our bedroom. While Hakeem, Devin and I sat up watching re-runs of Golden Girls and eating some midnight snacks. Hakeem was honestly a joy to be around and was a lot like his brother, just slightly more rugged, urban, and hood! He was truly the epitome of an Omega.

Devin went home around 11:30pm and it was time for me to get ready for bed. I handed Hakeem some fresh towels and a bottle of Dove from the linen closet.

After I showered, I was about to make myself comfortable but I stopped in the kitchen to grab 2 glasses of water to sit by Rakim and I's bedside. What I saw next almost gave me a damn heart-attack. Devin was right, Hakeem was too damn fine.

He had just gotten out of the shower so he only was wearing a towel that was wrapped around his waist but you could still see the crack of his perfectly toned ass. My heart melted and my panties got wet. I don't know if he was still wet or had just put on some type of oil but his body was shining from head to toe!

"And lead us not into temptation" I recited to myself. I'd learned that helped suppress any urges that may occur. I mean I had Rakim who was just as fine, but damn! Hakeem literally looked like a model from a fitness magazine. I had to go wipe myself. And put on a fresh pair of panties.

Maybe this wasn't such a good idea...

To be continued...

PART 17

"Fraternal Fantasy"

-Tacara

I've tried, and I've tried my best to stay away but I couldn't. The reason I hadn't been around in a while is because Destiny and Dr. Drew had honestly figured out some methods to suppressing me and her sexual tendencies. Which meant damn near deleting me for good. But I don't know what it was, but I came back this night. Keep in mind, I see, and hear everything that goes on. I'm always there, I just don't always make myself visible.

I creeped out of bed slowly and decided I needed to get laid. Or should I say, "we" needed it.

I crept to the back of the closet, quietly and pulled out the skank-est, most thot-ish outfit I could find. Rakim was knocked out cold, because ever since his accident, he'd become slightly addicted to pain pills for his back.

I sprayed a little Sweet Pea body spray on from Bath & Body works, slipped on a tight-fitted, sheer black laced dress, with some red Jessica Simpson pumps. The dress showed off my cleavage perfectly. I took off her glasses, took off her beautiful ring, teased my hair, and added just a touch of makeup. Well, let me not lie, I added a lot of make-up, I wanted to look extra slutty tonight. It'd been too damn long. I wasn't trying to make love tonight, I needed to get downright FUCKED!

I left the house, by putting the car in neutral and letting it roll out of the drive way quietly, so that I wouldn't wake the boys. One the car made it to the street, I crank it and turned the lights on.

I made it to the Hard Rock casino and the boys were out! I'm not really sure if there was some type of event or something but men were everywhere and me and my pussy were too excited!

I sat down at the Center-bar and ordered me a Peach Long-Island Iced Tea. It was so strong and gave me a buzz after just a couple of sips. Destiny's body was a light-weight.

After about 20 minutes of me playing on the machines and losing money, a fine gentleman walked up and asked if I had a light.

"Naw boo, sorry I don't smoke." I replied.

"Me either, I honestly just wanted to find some way to speak to you." He said nervously.

It was a cute attempt but he looked too innocent for me, and I almost brushed him off but the tailored suit and bulge in his pants turned me on. Brother was brown-skin, about 6'4, 170-180, clean cut dreads, with some pretty ass teeth, and a small birth mark on his right cheek. I had a thing for freckles and birth marks.

"So are you here on business or pleasure?" He asked nonchalantly.

"Pleasure. Just came to lose a couple dollars, and have a few drinks I guess..." I responded flirtatiously.

"Well here, maybe this will be good luck." He smiled and handed me a $100 dollar bill. "Try the Mr. Cashman machine, he's my favorite."

I gladly took his money and followed him to the machine. I examined how freaking gorgeous he was on the way there, even his walk was perfect. And there was just something about a brother with clean-cut dreads, especially with blonde just on the tips, and you could tell they were freshly re-twisted.

After I won $250 off of the $100 he gave me, I offered his money back but he refused and I wasn't going to argue with that. I slipped the money right in my bosom.

"So what brings you here, to the coast?" I asked.

"Is it that obviously that I'm not from here?" He asked.

"Yep, the tailored suit in the summer time lets me know you're here on business, your articulation, mixed with hood boy, let's me know you haven't always had much, but you've worked hard to get where you are now, the dreads and skin that looks softly kissed by the sun lets me know your people are from an island, and your shadow on your ring finger lets me know your married or used to be." I nailed it!

"Damn girl, you're good. And right. I'm from the Caribbean islands, and no, we were poor growing up but I've spent my entire life to make things better for my parents and siblings that are still on the island. I'm here for a leadership conference and my wife and I are separated at the moment. Anything else you can tell just from looking at me?"

"Yep, you want to make love to me. Don't you?" I asked.

"Nope, you're so wrong..." He smiled.

"Oh really, you don't?"

"No ma'am, I wanna fuck the shit out of you! No strings attached. Just let me lay this Caribbean dick on you and send you home to your man." He said aggressively and I was turned on to the max. "I have a room right upstairs. Meet me there in 10 minutes, here's my card key, room 1738."

"Okay, but I want to role-play." I responded. "I want to be your whore for tonight and I want you to pretend to rape me. Pin me down, feed me that big dick until I scream for mercy!"

"Rape huh? I don't know that sounds risky and crazy.. You into that kind of freaky shit?" He asked with a look of confusion.

"Yep, so take me! Fuck me good and long and hard! You ready?" I asked. "I'm trying to be your sex slave for a couple hours." I liked my lips.

"Does it look like I'm ready?" He asked as we both looked down at his dick print through this slacks.

"See you in 10..."

I used his hotel key card and walked into his hotel suite where he was standing there butt ass naked. His dick looked like a damn elephant trunk. I was starting think this wasn't such a good idea. But my panties being soaked was telling me otherwise.

He walked up to me and tied his tie over my mouth to muffle my screams and moans. He slipped off my dress and panties and began fingering me from behind aggressively. He lifted my left led on the bed, and bent down and ate me out like I was a damn buffet. I felt myself cum in his mouth, as I stroked my own clit and caressed my nipples. I moaned and he grabbed my hair and whispered, "Did I say you could moan, shut up!"

I came again. His deep voice turned me on. And his breath smelled like sweet mint.

He then turned the lights off and slammed me to the bed laying me flat on my stomach. Then he cuffed my thighs and spread them just enough to where he could forcefully enter me! It hurt so good!

"Ahhhh" I moaned loudly and he yanked my hair and said, "shut the fuck up and take this dick!"

He then continued to push deeper inside of me but something didn't feel right! I felt a strong pressure in my cervix that wasn't quite sensational. But painful! I moaned loud and tried to push him off of me, from behind but he kept going! Thinking it was part of the role-playing. I felt my insides literally ripping as he rammed all his inches inside of me repeatedly! I tried to push him off over and over but he continued to go and even covered my mouth with his hand although I couldn't be heard from the tie wrapped around my mouth!

I needed him to stop! Tears began rolling down my face and the pain became unbearable!

I scratched and cried out! But he didn't stop! I cuffed the sheets as the pain became too much!

I tried to scoot away but he pulled my body back and continued to plow inside of me!

I felt my body literally shutting down! I didn't know what was happening to me, it felt like death!

When he came inside of me, I laid there not moving, lifeless.

He rolled off of me and said: "is that how you wanted it baby?"

I didn't reply. I was unconscious.

He pulled back the sheets and blood was everywhere!

"Holy fuck! Oh my fucking! What the hell! Aye wake up! Wake up! Baby wake up!!! I'm sorry! I thought that's what you wanted!"

I didn't respond, my body was stiff and lifeless, and my pulse was weak...

To be continued...

PART 18

"Fraternal Fantasy"

-Destiny

"What's happening? Where am I? Who the hell are y'all!!?" I screamed, trying to wiggle my way off the hospital gurney strolling down the hall way. I looked up and the only thing I could see were men in white, bright lights, a police officer and my mom.

"What's happening? Can somebody say something! Was I in an accident?!" I yelled as my mom held my hand. "Mom tell me what's happening!"

"Baby, you'll be fine... Calm down." She said fighting back tears.

Something was terribly wrong, I could feel it all through my body!

Tears streamed from my face! My body was in some horrific pain, my head ached, my body had the chills, and my vagina felt like it had been ripped apart. Something was definitely wrong with me. But what?

"Was I raped?"

After being sedated I woke up to my mother, my brother Devin, and Rakim standing around my bed. Their eyes lit up when my eyes opened!

"Are you okay baby?" Rakim hurriedly yelled out.

"Don't crowd her Kim, let me talk to her first..." My mom replied to him. "Kim" was a nickname she'd given him in the past few months, and I don't think he liked it too much.

"Y'all what happened?" I asked with dry mouth, barely being able to speak.

Devin put a cup of water to my lips so that I could sip from the straw out of the hospital cup.

"Baby, you were in an accident..." My mom said before being interrupted by a detective.

"Ms. Destiny? Would you mind if I asked you a couple questions?" The black female officer asked.

"Sure, I guess, but I don't know anything, but can I finish talking with my mother first." I responded.

"Well, I'm Detective Yvette, I'm here to help you. Would you guys mind leaving the room for a moment?" She directed the question to my family.

"No, I have nothing to hide, this is my family and my fiancé. We all need to know what's going on." I replied but from the look on their faces, I think I was the only one in the dark.

"Tell me Destiny, what do you remember from last night?" Detective Yvette asked.

I struggled to sit up in the bed, to make myself more comfortable to speak.

"Well, I cooked dinner, my brother in law, Hakeem moved in with my fiancé and me. So after he was settled in, I, he, and my brother watched TV until we fell asleep. Devin left the house around 11. I took a shower, made 2 glasses of water for my fiancé and me, and then went to my room. The last thing I remember was getting in bed with my husband a little after 12am. Now can someone tell me what happened?" I replied eagerly.

Rakim interjected!

"When I woke up, you weren't there baby! I was a nervous wreck!" He exclaimed! "What made you leave the house without telling me, we don't have secrets...?"

Little did he know? -I thought to myself.

"Are you sure you don't want them leave the room?" She asked.

"I'm positive! Now can you please tell me what the heck is going on?! Sorry momma..." I never sworn in front of her.

"Well. We think you may have been taken advantage of last night. You were found unconscious in a hotel room at the Hard Rock casino." The detective said while flipping through her note pad.

"That's impossible. I never left my house, I don't gamble, and I definitely wouldn't be caught dead having sex! Who was he? How'd he know me, was a kidnapped?! Momma what's going on?!" I began to cry because everything was so blurry and inconclusive. But at the same time, I felt guilty, nasty, and responsible.

"Excuse us..." My mom said to my brother and Rakim.

"I'll be right outside the door baby, I'm here if you need me." Rakim replied, then kissed me on my forehead.

They left the room, and I looked at my mom whose eyes were filled with tears.

"Baby, it's time we discuss the blackouts." My mom replied.

"Blackouts?" The detective asked suspiciously.

"Yes, ever since she was a child she'd have these episodes where she forgot chunks of her life at a time. I never thought to get help because I figured it would get better with time. But it hasn't." My mom began to cry.

"Momma, wait, so you knew about my blackouts this entire time?! And you never told me! I've been going crazy and probably could've been killed last night and you never mentioned it to me! Momma why?" I slowly moved my hand away from hers with the feeling of betrayal.

"Baby, it's a long story. But you're old enough to know the truth now. Dr. Drew will be here shortly." She replied.

"What about the rape? Who was he? And how'd he find me! I know I have blackouts but I didn't I could drive or do anything during them! Do you think I've had sex before? Oh my God! What's happening to me?" I asked aloud, feeling ashamed and sinful.

"The gentleman is in custody but he claims everything was consensual. Do you remember him at all?" The detective asked, while handing me a picture of his mugshot.

The tears went into overtime. I cried so hard! Everything in my mind and heart told me to say: "no I don't know him, let him rot in jail and hell for what he did to me," but that wasn't the case.

I got quiet for a second. Feeling like I could remember face from a dream or memory from long ago.

"What's wrong Destiny? Is this the man, tell me what happened? I need to know?!" The detective asked aggressively.

I was too choked up to speak. Tears and snot streamed from my face. My body was in pain, I couldn't remember anything but the picture of that man triggered something inside of me. A familiar feeling.

"Let him go." I cried out softly. "He didn't rape me?"

"But there's evidence that......" I cut the detective off.

"Please detective, just listen to me. I wasn't raped. Let the man go... I can't explain what happened but I know he didn't rape me." She looked confused but had no choice but leave my room, making a phone call to release the innocent man.

It felt just like the nurse from that night in Rakim's hospital room. Or so many other men I've seen in my life. I literally couldn't remember being with them, but something inside of me did.

To be continued...

PART 19

"Fraternal Fantasy"

-Destiny

I was released from the hospital the following day and more than anything I just wanted to be alone. So many unanswered questions went through my head, and I was literally beginning to think I was going crazy. Imagine attempting to "save yourself for marriage" and all of that being taken away in one night? It didn't make sense to me. I've never been promiscuous, but I knew that man didn't take advantage of me.

What was happening to my body?

There were a lot of things going on in my life: the wedding, the black outs, the rape, Hakeem moving in, and on top of all of that I would be returning to work soon. I didn't know exactly which way to turn, so of course, I did what most people do in these circumstances. I asked my mom to come stay with us for a while. Just until things were back to normal. Or until I felt mentally and physically equipped to deal with everyday life.

Of course Rakim nor Hakeem objected to her staying for a few nights, but it was still slightly overwhelming to be young people, with one of our mothers around. But I knew it was what I needed.

When I returned to work she took care of all the duties as far as house chores, cooking, and even helping me out with lesson plans. I would come home to full course meals like when I was in middle school, and even freshly washed and ironed clothes. She adores basketball, so she and the guys would stay up for hours gossiping and janking each other about who was greater out of LeBron and Kobe. She made everything seem so much better. I was so blessed to have her.

It was a Friday night and I was looking forward to the weekend, wedding planning with Bri & Jaleisa, and also spending some much needed time with my baby and my mom.

The girls and I met at Bri's new apartment, and discussed colors, cakes, and dresses. There was one thing about my girls, they always had my back. But sometimes I wondered had they ever experienced my blackouts and never told me? Or had I possibly been the topic of discussion among guys on campus? Or was I just overthinking everything? One thing was for sure, and that's that I was driving myself damn near insane.

I needed some much needed mother-daughter time.

Once I made it home, Hakeem and Rakim were both passed out in the spare room or what they called the "man-cave," so I quietly shut the door to go chat with my mom and watch some re-runs.

"Baby, I think it's time we set the appointment with Dr. Drew again, but this time I should be there." My mom exclaimed in the middle of our favorite episode of Law & Order.

"I know ma, but things are just starting to get back to normal and honestly, since you've been here, I haven't had any black outs or missed out on any events that may or may not have taken place." I explained.

"I understand that, but there's still some things that need to be discussed."

"Like what?" I asked placing my soda back on the coffee table.

"See... Well..." She paused.

"What is it momma, just talk to me..." I explained, reaching out for her hand.

"There's something you should know about your father Destiny, before this gets out of hand, I have to tell you what really happened the night your father died." My heart felt like it was about to explode. I looked at her with confusion.

"What do you mean? What happened? It was a car accident right? That's what you've told me all these years, that's what I remember! Are you telling me that something else happened to him?" I was destroyed, I felt every bone in my body filled with rage and anger. The last thing I needed to find out is that my mother was a liar!

"Calm down Destiny, just listen to me."

"I'm listening..."

"Have you ever wondered why there's no pictures of you before the age of ten? Or why your brothers and I barely ever mention anything from the past?" She asked sincerely.

"Deshaun told me it's because it would make me cry when I was younger to see pictures of dad. He said it was to protect me. He told me he and Devin destroyed all the photos to help me get over the loss of dad..." I exclaimed.

"Do you remember him, or anything before the age of 10, at all?" She asked.

I pondered the idea. I pictured his face vaguely in my mind before answering her question. I tried to remember what it felt like before the night I found out he was gone.

But I couldn't. I could feel my body becoming numb and emotionless. I could tell I was about to black out. Never had it happened in this type of situation, but it was clear that my inner emotions were triggering my loss of time.

"Destiny? Destiny? Are you okay?!" My mom shook me rapidly.

"It's happening mom, don't let me leave your sight! I can feel myself fading, don't let me do anything stupid..." I replied as I felt myself drifting off, almost into a state of slumber.

"Baby! Wait! Talk to me! What's making this happen?!"

-Tacara

I was filled with anger and rage! Due to recent events people only noticed the bad things I've done in Destiny's body, completely forgetting that I'm the reason those memories are gone! I saved her, I'm her protector! No one was going to ruin the protection I had for her.

"Did you really think it was a good idea to disclose that type of information to her, especially right now?" I asked Ms. Johnson with a smirk.

I took off Destiny's glasses to give her a better look at who I really was.

"Who are you?" She asked squinting her eyes with confusion.

"You know exactly who I am! Please don't act like you don't... Can you do me a favor and just please not tell her what happened! It would kill her! Trust me! I'm the only reason those memories are gone, because I hold them inside!" I explained.

"I don't understand, are you a demon, a spirit? Or just Destiny playing some sick joke?! Who are you...?" She asked while pushing back my bangs to get a better look at my face. As if it changed drastically just from removing Destiny's glasses.

"I'm her protector. I've been her protector since birth! And all through our child hood, look at me! Who do you think I am?!" I asked with tears forming in my eyes.

"What do you mean? You look like my daughter? You look like Destiny!" She expressed!

"Look harder, I mean really look at me!" I took a deep breath and let out a sigh.

She squinted her eyes and gasped with her hand over her mouth!

"TACARA?!" She whispered as chills went up her arms, and her face turned pale as if she had just seen a ghost.

To be continued...

PART 20

"Fraternal Fantasy"

-Tacara

"Yes, it's me... I never left, I've been here all along." I expressed to her while caressing her hand.

"I don't understand... Destiny has never mentioned anything about you. It's been 14 years and she's never even given me a clue that she knew about you..." She replied.

"And she still doesn't know about me. It's hard to explain, but when she hurts, I hurt. So from a young age I vowed to never let anyone hurt her, ever again. So even now, I stop any and every negative entity that comes her way..." I started to become choked up and let my emotions get the best of me. Because I let my guard go, Destiny's stress level had returned to normal. Which means her defense mechanism, me, went away. I felt myself drift away and my eyesight faded. Destiny was coming back...

-Destiny

"Momma why are you crying? Momma..." I shook her shoulder and wiped the tears from her eyes. "Momma, what happened?"

"Nothing baby, you're perfect. You are simply perfect honey." She replied putting my glasses back on my face and kissing me on the forehead.

The next morning I woke up to my mom's bags packed with a full breakfast made fresh. Turkey bacon, pancakes, eggs, with freshly squeezed orange juice. I knew there was something she wasn't telling me, but I didn't want to press the issue and cause myself to stress and fade out again.

"Bags? What's this? Momma I know you're not leaving us?" Rakim exclaimed in disappointment while grabbing a peace of turkey bacon off the counter.

"Yes baby boy, but I'll be back soon, I promise." She replied to him then looked at me. "Don't forget, we have an appointment with Dr. Drew next Monday."

"That's the day before the wedding momma, no ma'am, can we postpone it?" I asked while pushing my plate away from the loss of my appetite.

"Destiny Renee, what did I say?! There's some things that need to be discussed before the wedding. Just to go into your marriage with a clear mind, body and soul. And because I said so!" She shouted. And Rakim chuckled. He always thought it was funny when my mom got on to me and the boys.

"I don't know why you're laughing, you'll be there too." My mom darted the response to Rakim who had scrambled eggs on his top lip.

"Huh, who me? Oh no ma'am, I would've never passed Psychology had I not cheated off my line brother. Is it okay if I pass this one time? I'm not good with head doctor stuff." Rakim replied.

"No, you'll be there..." My mom replied picking up her keys and purse and kissing both of us on the foreheads.

"Ugh yes ma'am.." Rakim replied.

That week had to be one of the most stressful times of my life. I don't know if I'd mentioned but we had to cram the wedding because Rakim wanted it to be the same day as his parents wedding. Which was fine with me.

Honestly, I was the type of girl that had always dreamed of an amazing wedding. Not to mention my line-sisters and Devin had pretty much taking care of most of the arrangements and invites. I was content.

We'd picked the beach front to have the ceremony. Simple, cute, quick, with the colors of our Greek lives. My brother Deshaun was in charge of the music, Hakeem in charge of making sure their side of the family could make it, and of course Devin took care of the decor and attire.

It was definitely going to be a wedding to remember.

The week progressed well and even with all the stress I'd maintained to stay completely alert and avoiding any blackouts. My house was full of men who protected me at all times, so I was pretty sure I was taken care of. Due to the wedding planning, Devin and Deshaun had pretty much moved in for the week. Which was like having four grown kids in the house at all times. They played video games, cards, and argued about basketball 24/7.

Monday morning came and I dreaded the fact of having my future husband and mother seeing a Psych doctor with me. Although I didn't have many secrets, that I knew of.

"Ready baby?" I asked Rakim as he slid on his Cole Haans.

"Waiting on you princess, let's roll." He waved his hand and headed towards the door.

We got in the car and our favorite church song began playing. Although we had two different religious beliefs, we found some common ground when it came to believing in a higher power. It was interesting hearing he and Hakeem talk about Muhammad, and their beliefs.

But there was nothing that could change my thoughts on the man who died on the cross for me.

We pulled up to Dr. Drew's office and my mom was already inside.

"Dr. Drew and your mom have been waiting on you two love birds.." The receptionist said and Rakim and I looked at each other crazy.

I'm guessing my mom had blabbed about us getting married to literally everyone but the Pope.

"Morning guys, can I get y'all something to drink?" Dr. Drew asked us.

"I'm fine, thank you ma'am."

"Me too, I'm good."

"I'll take a water," my mom said quietly. There wasn't many times she showed emotions but this was definitely a time for it. I could see it all over her face. Something was truly bothering her.

"So who wants to speak first?" Dr. Drew asked, but looked directly at me.

"Ummm, I guess I will since I am the common denominator in the room..." They chuckled.

"Well, as everyone knows I've been having black outs for quite some time now. And I just want to start by saying they've gotten better thanks to the people in this room, but I honestly feel like there's something I don't know. That obviously everyone else does. I feel left out. I just want to go into my marriage with no secrets, so is there something I should know? If so, just tell me mom. What is it about dad you didn't want to mention the other night? Was he not my real dad? I'll never judge you, I just want to know the truth and if this has anything to do with what's happening to me now." I said, looking down and twirling my thumbs nervously.

My mom took a sip of her water but didn't speak... She was extremely nervous.

"Well baby, like I told you before, I'm behind you 100% but I just want to know what triggers them, so we can avoid them all cost. Doctor, isn't there some kind of medication that can help with that?" Rakim asked as if he wouldn't mind me walking around doped up. I guess he felt anything was better than me wondering the streets at all times of night.

"There are medications but we don't want to take that route unless it's necessarily. Which I don't think it is. It's important that we get to the route of the problem. Ms. Johnson, I'm guessing there's something you want to discuss with us this morning?" Dr. Drew pushed up her glasses and looked in my mother's direction.

"Yes, there is something I need to say. But I'm not sure where to start." My mom said nervously and sounding as if she was about to cry...

"It's okay Momma, just talk to us." I tried to calm her down.

"Start from the beginning..." Dr. Drew informed her as we all sat anxiously waiting...

To be continued.

PART 21

"Fraternal Fantasy"

-Destiny

The room got so quiet that the only thing you could hear were the deep breaths being taken and the sounds of my mom sniffling. Whatever she was holding inside was festering deep within her and stressing her out to the max. It was time to reveal whatever it was. And honestly, I was starting to think Deshaun and Devin should have been there, instead of Rakim. But it was too late now. I looked over at him and he looked more nervous than anyone. Poor guy, probably felt like he bit off more than he could chew by getting engaged to me. But if we could make it through this, we could possibly make it through anything.

"Is there any circumstances that would make you obligated to contact the police from the information I'm about to disclose?" My mom asked Dr. Drew.

"Only if the information jeopardizes your life or the life of someone else. Other than that, it stays between the people in this room. That being said, I recommend the information shared today, to never leave this room..." She replied, looking down at her recorder.

"Momma, is it that serious? Should Rakim be here?" I looked over at him.. "And why did you chose to come do this in front of Dr. Drew if it was such a big family matter?" I asked, pondering in ideas and becoming more frustrated and confused by the second.

"Because it includes everyone in this room..." My mom replied and Dr. Drew's face turned pale and emotionless. "Dr. Drew and Rakim too..."

"Me? I never knew Destiny before the day we met."
Rakim replied.

Dr. Drew then pressed the stop-button on the recorder.

"Denise do you really think that's best?" Dr. Drew firmly
asked my mom. She went from patient-client, to home
girls real quick.

"Wait you two know each other?" I asked with
confusion.

"Yes, let me explain..." Dr. Drew said with empathy.

"Yes! Please, somebody tell me something! So Dr. Drew
did you tell my mom the things we discussed? And if so,
how much?" I asked, wondering if she'd mentioned my
ideas of sex but never actually having it, to my
knowledge. Or would Rakim know I touched him that
night in the hospital?

"Nothing, we haven't discussed you, since you were a
child." She responded.

"Yes, baby, she's right. Once you became of age, I no
longer was allowed to know the things you talked about.
But right after the accident, Dr. Drew was your
Psychiatric Pediatrician." My mom said looking up at Dr.
Drew.

I looked up at Dr. Drew and even after all of our one-on-
one sessions, I began to finally recollect vague memories
of her. I could remember a younger version of her with
the same type of glasses and hairstyle. The memories of
her was causing my emotions to become overwhelmed.
So I closed my eyes and meditated. I felt a black out
coming but this time I was determined to fight it! I had to
hear what was going on.

Dr. Drew could tell the blackout was coming and began to sing:

"Amazing Grace, how sweet the sound that saved a wretch like me.... I once was lost but now I'm found, was blind by now I seeeee" Dr. Drew's voice was like a magic trick. I instantly became calm from the sound of her voice.

My mom then turned to me, and placed her hand on my knee.

"Baby, okay, I need you to know I love you very much, and what I am about to tell you was for your own good. It was your 10th birthday party. I had dressed you up in the cutest little pink and yellow polka-dotted dress, and your hair was in pigtails with yellow bows on each braid. Your brother Devin, only 13 at the time, had taken the liberty of making you this amazing triple chocolate cake that he was so proud of. And also matched all the decorations to the polka dots on your dress. Your happiness has always been his motivation for living. And Deshaun, oh my baby, had stayed up all night making you a soundtrack of all of your favorite songs at the time. I need you to understand that your brothers knew what I'm about to tell you. But since it was such a young age, we were advised it would be best to tell you when you got older. That's why I'm here today." She began to get choked up and so was I. Thinking about the fact that the birthday party she was explaining, was so similar to my wedding plans.

I loved my brothers so much...

She grabbed a tissue off of Dr. Drew's desk, wiped her eyes, and went on with her story...

To be continued...

PART 22

"Fraternal Fantasy"

-Destiny

My mom continued with the story as Rakim, Dr. Drew and myself pictured all the events she was reminiscing on. I looked around the room and everyone was crying, even Rakim, and I never thought I'd see that day. And Dr. Drew was supposed to be used to this kind of stuff, but she was a ball of tears and emotions. And words can't express the anxiety I felt for whatever my mom was about to tell me.

"Your father had a terrible drinking problem that started once he got out of the military. It caused so many problems and I threatened to leave him, but I couldn't bear the thought of losing my husband or depriving my children of their father.

He became verbally disrespectful and physically abusive, which is why your brother Deshaun is so protective of you and I, he would literally fist fight your father to stop him from attacking us. But the abuse went to an entirely different level once you told me that he had been touching you. And it wasn't that I didn't believe you, I just thought you may have misinterpreted the father-daughter relationship you had. Or just wanted him to leave us alone. But I didn't think I could raise all of you on my own! I'm so sorry Destiny! I wanted to believe you baby, I wanted to! But I couldn't imagine someone hurting my babies so I ignored you. Time and time again." She began to cry so hard and there wasn't a dry eye in the room.

We could all feel the pain she was displaying. I wanted to reach out to console her but there was something gilding me back. It wasn't that I was mad, but I did feel some sort of resentment towards her, if what she was saying was indeed true.

My emotions were sky-rocketing but I didn't feel faint. Whatever usually came over me had suppressed itself, which further let me know I needed to hear the rest of my mom's story.

She wiped her nose, and continued.

"The day of your birthday was different though. I could feel something was wrong. There were kids from all over the neighborhood there that day, but when I looked around for you. You were nowhere to be found, and neither was your father. I looked all around the yard, but there was no sight of you. I walked down the hall way and I could feel the tension of hurt, lies, and fear in the air. I felt like something was going wrong. My palms were sweating, my heart was racing and my body felt weak... I slowly turned the knob on your bedroom door and there you stood with your father's loaded 9 mm pistol that he kept on the closet shelf. By the time I reached out to grab the gun from you, you had taken both of your small precious hands and fired off into your father's back. I tried to stop you, but it was too late...."

"Whh-what? Momma no.... No... That didn't happen?" I shook my head rapidly back and forth. "So you're saying I killed daddy? But why? How? I can't even shoot a gun now? What if I was just young and lying about being molested? What made me pull the trigger?!" I was devastated! Tears fell down my face like a waterfall.

"You had to baby, you had to..." She struggled to talk through the hurt and tears.

"But why momma? Why?!"

"Baby I have to tell you one more thing and please don't hate me for keeping it from you. Please baby girl...... But, I ummm," she paused for a second and took a deep breath.

"I didn't just have one set of twins, I had 2 sets. One set of boys, and 3 years later a set of girls." I could barely understand her through the crackling and tears in her voice.

"What happened to the girls? Where are they now?" I asked. It wasn't really making sense... It is was too much!

"The day of your birthday, you walked in your bedroom to find your father on top of your sister. You shot him in his back, and the bullet went through him, and killed her too..."

"Who? Who did I kill?!" I couldn't even think straight! I was taking in too much information at one time! My heart felt like it was going to pound of my chest! "Who was she momma?"

She then pulled out an old photo of 2 young, identical, black girls, with pink dresses, yellow polka dots, and yellow ribbons on their pigtails. I rubbed my hand across the faces of the girls and every memory of my childhood came flooding back. Suddenly, I remembered everything about that day. She was trying to stop him from raping me, got aggressive, beat her, and raped her instead. I went and found the gun and meant to just kill him. But I killed my sister too. I rubbed her face on the photo as if to say I was sorry...

"*Tacara......*" I whispered...

To be continued...

PART 23

"Fraternal Fantasy"

-Destiny

With a heavy heart, I looked around the room and noticed everyone starting at me. It didn't make sense? How could my mom have kept these secrets from me for so long? And Devin couldn't hold water, I couldn't believe he hadn't told me sooner. I was lost, I was hurt, I was a murderer. Everything felt like a lie. Or some type of fairy tale fantasy.

Could I really live with a multiple-personality?

I felt Rakim rub my back to console me.

"I really think I should step out for a minute and let you and your mom talk.." Rakim said sincerely.

"No baby, stay... I need you. You're the only thing that makes sense right now..." I replied then looked up at my mom who was staring at the picture of Tacara and myself.

"Why didn't you just tell me? I've been going crazy all these years. The blackouts were just the least of my problems; compared to how it felt to be missing my complete other half. I've always felt alone momma. You're great, my brothers are amazing, but there was always something missing... Why didn't you tell me?" I asked.

"Baby I wanted to, I tried on so many occasions but each and every time I brought it up, you became so emotional. You've always been extra sensitive. I wanted to wait until the timing was right. I knew I would have to tell you someday about Tacara, but just not under these circumstances." She looked down at the picture once more, and although she was still crying, she smiled a little.

"What's funny?" I asked, wiping the tears from my eyes.

"When I was pregnant with you two, I had major complications in the beginning of the pregnancy, the doctor told me one of you may not make it from lack of food and nutrients." She replied.

"It's called Twin-to-Twin Transfusion Syndrome." Dr. Drew interjected.

"That's it, one of the two of you weren't going to make it, but after a couple months the more dominant twin had completely switched positions and allowed the other to receive all the proper food intake that was needed. It's almost like she sensed that you were getting weak. The night you two were born, Tacara came first. She didn't cry, she didn't scream, they thought something may have been wrong with her. But she was fine and healthy. She was 6 lbs. and 4 ounces. After the doctors suctioned and cleaned her off she opened her eyes just as bright and ready for the world, still no tears. Just looking around the room, like she'd been here before. But you, you were different. 16 minutes later, you came out screaming! 5 lbs. 6 ounces, hollering! The doctors and nurses ran in circles attempting to calm you down. Nothing worked. They cleaned you off, suctioned you and you were still screaming to the top of your lungs. Finally I got the chance to hold quiet Tacara in my left arm, and screaming Destiny in my right. You opened your eyes and looked directly at her and your tears stopped." My mom began to cry again. But tears of joy and remembrance.

"Really momma?" I smiled through the pain.

"Yes baby, and it didn't stop there. She was always able to make you feel calm and comfortable growing up. That girl was something fierce when it came to you. Your first day of head start, Tacara came home with dirt all over her clothes, scratches on her knees, and all of her bows missing from her hair. She'd beat up a kid on the first day! I was so upset with her. Until she told me it was because someone called you 'four-eyes' and made you cry. She was always your protector."

My mother telling me all of the memories of my childhood made me feel somewhat better about everything I'd been through. I was still lost and felt slightly hurt, but to know my sister still lived within me made me feel like I wasn't alone.

"So Dr. Drew how do we fix this? I mean, how do I let her go?" I asked with a look of concern.

"It's hard to say. You've formed an emotional bound with the spirit of your twin sister." Dr. Drew responded. "The bond twins share is a phenomenon. Twins form bonds early on in the womb and all through their lives. I'm sure you can tell from your brothers."

"So is it real? Or is it just something I'm doing to myself? I mean, I've done my share of psychological research, and these types of situations are mostly inconclusive? What do you suggest?" I asked.

"I suggest you find a way to live together. Accept the fact that you are two people, in one. If you've done your share of studies, you should know that this is in fact common. People live with multiple-personalities every day. It's up to you to figure out how you'll deal with it." She replied and I turned to look at Rakim.

"So, I'm guessing we should probably postpone the wedding? Right?" I asked.

He looked me right in my eyes.

"For what? I love you. All of you. Like I said before, this is all new to me. But it's new to you too baby. Let's learn how to deal with it together. We'll do our research and I'll do everything in my power to show 'Tacara' that I can protect you now, so she can rest in peace. I love you baby." Rakim said while reaching over to kiss me softly.

I sighed.

"I love you too Rakim, and thank you for supporting me through this..." I replied.

"Tomorrow I want to make you my wife. Through sickness and health. For better or worse. Tacara and all... Let's do this baby girl."

To be continued.

PART 24

"Fraternal Fantasy"

-Destiny

Guess what today is? The day every girl dreams of. The day when nothing goes wrong. The day you give your all to someone that makes you feel worthy!

It's my Wedding Day!

After the tragic day before, I spent countless hours talking to my brother Devin about everything from our childhood up until recent events. He was very caring and understanding, but mostly wanted me to focus on today. He was worse than any girl I'd ever met when it came to weddings or anything that dealt with pretty colors and dresses.

I woke up that morning completely blissful. A couple members of his family had come in but no sight of his mother, who mentioned she may or may not come due to my non-converting. But that was okay, he was happy and so was I. Just for this one day, I wanted to forget about everything and start a new life with the man of my dreams.

My house had never been filled with so many people. Everyone but my future husband. Rakim, Hakeem, Deshaun, and a few of Rakim's Line-brothers went out the night before and decided it'd be best to rent out the hotel suite for the day to get ready there.

I woke up at 6AM for a hair appointment with Jamal Thomas. He braided my natural hair to my scalp, and then gave me a sew-in of 4 bundles of 24-inch Malaysian. Then styled it perfectly, it was so pretty! My hair was completely laid! I looked like a princess. Once he was finished I rushed to Krystal Towner's to have my face put on. She had given me a complete make-over! After that, I was a gorgeous, devastating diva about to marry my perfect Kappa man.

Because of our religious differences, our wedding was non-traditional & non-domination. We decided to let a mutual friend officiate our wedding. Needless to say, his family, nor mine was entirely okay with our decision, but with everything that had taken place, I was eager to marry my husband, and create a future with him.

I arrived on the beach around 3:30. The sun was perfect, the chairs were filled with guest, and there were even plenty of people standing around.

My dress was a soft, pure white linen Zara dress, with a single-strand red belt. My breast looked perfect, because it showed just enough cleavage. I had on red Steve Madden pumps, with a small strap around my ankle that made calve muscles look amazing. I was simple, but simplicity was exactly what I needed.

I pulled up in the limo, and one of Rakim's line brothers opened the door for me. He looked amazing as well. Instead of the traditional 4-6 groomsmen, Rakim had every line brother that crossed with him initially, which meant 13 Kappas, my brother Deshaun, and his brother Hakeem. It looked like a page out of an Ebony Magazine titled: "Mississippi's Finest!"

My side was slightly different. I didn't have a bridesmaid, because my best friend is my brother Devin. Who stood there in a white linen suit, with a red Ralph Lauren button down, He was so handsome. Behind him stood Bri. Who had totally outdone me. She had on a red dress, that eventuated every curve on her body and her breast were popping out! She must've had her eye on one of the groomsmen. All my other girls had on either white or red linen dress. And looked amazing as well.

As soon as one of my shiny, red pumps hit the sand, the entire congregation stood to their feet, and Devin began to sing, as I walked down the red carpet that had been laid out for me. Devin sang Mul-Ty (Looking for Love).

As I began to walk slowly with a beautiful bouquet of red and white flowers, I looked around at everyone looking back at me. For some reason the only people I noticed were the men, and although I may or may not have known them, they all seemed so familiar. Like I had met them in a dream. But I continued to walk.

As I gazed up, I noticed Rakim crying and Hakeem behind him rubbing his back supportively. It was an image I'll never try to erase. It was simply beautiful.

Once I made it to them, he took my hand and helped me on the hand-built gazebo. I wiped his tears.

"Dearly beloved, we are gathered here today. To join in matrimony these two beautiful people. Rakim Abdul, and Destiny Johnson will now be joined as one. The couple has prepared their own vows."

Rakim went first. Still choked up and tears falling slowly.

"I'm okay, I'm okay..." He shrugged Hakeem's hand off his shoulders and cleared his throat.

"You see how the sun is shining so bright on us today? How its shine brightened our day this morning, how its existence helps each creature on this earth nourish and grow? That's how your love is for me. You are my sunshine, my strength and my nourishment. I promise to love you through anything we ever endure. I want to grow old, wrinkled and out of shape with you, and I promise to love every inch. I want all your home girls to say, 'DAMN, they still together?!' Ms. Destiny, I have seen the best of you, the worst of you, and some parts of you I will never understand. But I love and accept you for all. I love you..."

By the time he finished, my makeup was ruined from tears, but I cleared my throat because it was my turn.

I smiled.

"Rakim, I don't ever want you to steal, lie, or cheat. But if you do steal, then steal away my sorrows, all my worries and my stress. If you do lie, then lie with me for all the days and nights of our lives, and if you must cheat. Please cheat death, so I don't ever have to imagine a day without you. Its sounds so cheesy to say, but baby you complete me. I always felt lost, angry, selfish, crazy, but then I met you and I felt whole again. You are the epitome of the perfect man. You get on my damn nerves sometimes, sorry momma, but I wouldn't have it any other way. I love you Rakim...."

After we finished, you could hear the soft cries and sniffles from everyone watching. Especially Devin, who was standing right behind me.

"Is there anyone that feels these two shouldn't be together today? If so, speak now or forever hold your peace..."

We both turned to the crowd, but the only person standing was the limo driver who was awkwardly watching and starring every hard.

"Anyone feel that these two should get married today, speak now!"

Everyone went crazy!

"Ooooooo-ooop!" My line sisters calked out, and "YO BABY YO BABY YOOOOO" from every Kappa on the beach! It was insane!

"I now pronounce you Husband and Wife. Mr. and Mrs. Rakim Abdul."

We kissed, and my knees got weak. I was married to the love of my life.

Rakim grabbed my hand as we walked back downward the aisle to get into the limo and meet everyone at the center for our reception. They began to play music, and everyone began to stroll.

We were smiling so hard, as everyone threw rice on us.

We got to the limo and the driver turned around to open the door, and then turned back to face us.

"Congratulations..." He said with a deep, raspy voice, while opening the door.

I squinted my eyes and felt a sharp pain in my stomach.

"DADDY?" I exclaimed before passing out into Rakim's arms.

To be continued...

PART 25

"Fraternal Fantasy"

-Destiny

I stood there in awe for about 5 seconds because there was something so familiar about this man. He looked just like my dad. But the memories I had of my father's death were beyond vivid! So it couldn't be! It just couldn't be I thought to myself.

"Daddy?" The limousine driver asked with confusion. "Ughh no ma'am, I ain't cha daddy." He replied with a southern slang.

"Never mind, I'm sorry.... It's been a long day." I replied faking a smile but still looking at all the dimensions of his face. There was something about him.

"Destiny, I love you baby, you are my wife and I promise to never disrespect you. But get your simple minded behind in this car so we can go to the hotel and I can show you a few things..." Rakim replied jokingly, while grabbing his dick through his pants.

"Okay baby..." I smiled, and sat next to him in the limo.

He began to kiss me seductively, and I ask the limo driver, "Role up the partition please"

As I kissed my husband and was about to make passionate love to him.

We arrived at the hotel suite and it was something of a fairy tale. I could tell from the colors and the Feng-shui of the room, Devin had sat all of this up. It was full of off-white furniture with gold trim and flowers all around. It had my favorite smell of vanilla filling the room, with Champaign on the rocks.

"Just give me a second okay." I lifted one finger to Rakim as I entered the bathroom to get ready. Just wanted to spruce my self up since I was about to "lose my virginity."

I took off my dress, let my hair down, and put on some sexy, red-laced lingerie Bri had picked out for me, particularly for this night. I softly sprayed a little bit of Bath & Body Work's Japanese Cherry Blossom on my crotch, and also added some lotion just for the places I knew he would kiss.

Now, I'm not sure if any of y'all are aware. But I am technically a virgin. As far as I know. I mean I'm sure there's some things Tacara has done in the past but this was my first time and I prayed she wouldn't appear and ruin it.

I slowly walked out of the bathroom and Rakim was lying on the bed with nothing but some black Ralph Lauren skin-tight briefs on. You could see how big his dick was from the way the bulge pointed downward like a damn hook in his underwear.

"Oh my God baby! You know how long I've been waiting for this moment?!" He asked anxiously!

"A long time baby, I know..." I replied while slipping off one of the straps to my bra.

"You damn right, 1 year, 8 months, 3 weeks, and 4 days to be exact, now come on..." We both laughed and he grabbed his dick to readjust himself.

I laid next to him, nervous. Because I had never had this happen without a blackout. But I honestly didn't even feel light headed. I guess Tacara felt like I was safe.

He leaned over and began to kiss my neck and my body began to shiver. The kisses felt soft, moist, and like he wanted me more than words can express. He took his tongue and licked all over my neck, my ears, and worked his way down to my breast.

I began to take off my pumps from the wedding but he insisted I keep them on.

I took off my bra, and let my breast hang as he softly kissed each of them. In all the excitement he was about to hop out of his underwear but I wanted him to wait. This was MY first time and I wanted it to be special.

"Stand up." I demanded.

He looked at me with one eye squinted.

"Like this?!" He asked, pointing at his dick that was fighting to get out of his briefs.

"Yes, Rakim stand up."

He stood there and it was the most majestic black man I had ever seen in my life. His chest bulged from his body with pure muscle, and although he was dark as midnight, but the areola around his nipples looked like dark Hershey kisses. He was shaved perfectly. Which was good, because I couldn't stand hairy men. His abs made me wet from their perfect structure. And he had a v-cut that stopped right where his underwear began. Even his thighs and feet were pretty.

I touched myself to make sure a black out wasn't coming and it didn't. It felt so good watching him stand there like a model and feeling on my own clit.

"Drop them." I announced.

"Destiny what? Why? Can I just get in the bed you sitting over there playing with yourself, can I at least come taste it!?" He asked with his sad puppy dog eyes."

"Drop them Rakim, take them off.." I repeated then he rolled his eyes with frustration and bent over slowly to take his underwear off.

He slid them down slowly, then kicked them onto the bed, almost hitting me in the face. His dick looked like a big, black, cucumber! It was huge with veins popping out everywhere.

"What's that?" I asked. Noticing some cum like substance hanging from his dick.

"Pre-nut... You wanna taste it?" He asked, shaking his dick in my direction. It looked so tasty!

"Come here." I motioned with my index finger.

He walked over, and I scooted to the edge of the bed. His dick was heavy. I lifted it and placed it in my mouth and began to suck on it. His pre-nut tasted sweet, like pineapple juice.

He began to moan! And grinding himself in and out of my mouth. He then took both of his hands and removed my bra while his dick was still in my mouth. It felt so good.

He caressed my nipples and I felt my pussy get wet. So wet, I could feel it on the bedsheets.

"Can I taste it?" He asked, and I immediately laid on my back and elevated my legs.

"Damn, you sure you ready for this?" He said licking his pretty, big lips.

I shook my head yes.

He took his thumb and index finger and opened my walls and inserted his tongue. It felt so good and I could feel myself moisturizer his mouth with my juices. My body was tingling from head to toe. He then took his tongue and swirled it all around my clit until I couldn't take it anymore.

"You like that huh?" He asked, and I'm sure my moaning spoke for itself.

He then stood up, dick standing at full attention, and then rubbed it on my clit.

"Can I go in?" He asked.

"Yes baby, be gentle."

He slid it in with ease and had a look of surprise on his face. I guess I wasn't as tight as he expected! That damn Tacara!

The pain was killing me but I took it anyway.

I threw my head back and began moaning like crazy. He drilled my insides and tried to cover his hand over my mouth but I just licked his fingers.

He began to go really fast, and I felt him hit a spot that I didn't want him to move from.

"Right there baby, keep going right there!" I moaned, but awkwardly I felt something I hadn't felt in weeks!

I think I was blacking out... "Tacara please not right now.." I thought to myself.

After a few minutes of the best moments of my entire life, I felt my body shivering! Pulsating and nutting everywhere!

"Where you want me to come?" Rakim asked smiling with sweat dripping down his face.

"In me..." I replied.

I felt his dick pulsating inside me, as he came.

I was about to get up, but "fuck it" I thought to myself.

"I want you to sleep inside of me..."

"Yes ma'am Mrs. Destiny.. I love you baby..." He replied, out of breath and kissing me softly.

-Tacara

I woke up with Rakim's sweaty ass on top of me! And lord knows I didn't want to ruin her wedding day, but that just wasn't enough for me. I scooted him off and out of me slowly. And went to the bathroom to finish off what he started. I grabbed a small porcelain figurine off the stand in the hotel and went to the bathroom. I lifted one leg on the sink top, and drilled myself with it until I came over and over again.

When I was finish, I looked at myself in the mirror and noticed how pretty Destiny was on her wedding day.

I kissed the mirror.

"I love you Destiny, congrats on your big day baby girl."

"I love you too Tacara..." I heard her say from inside me.

To be continued....

PART 26

"Fraternal Fantasy"

-Destiny

After an amazing night with my husband, I woke up the next day in total peace and bliss. Truth is. Although I couldn't see Tacara, I could actually feel her inside of me. It was weird, but growing up with twin brothers and being married to a twin, I needed the comfort of having her there. We would just have to come to an understanding when it came to her screwing whomever she pleased.

We woke up that day to all 3 of our brothers. They'd obviously had an entire day planned for us, but truth is, I just wanted to go home and rest. My mom and I had made plans for a full spa day and then take care of a couple things around my house.

Therefore the guys spent the entire day together doing
God knows what, while my mom and I spent the day
cooking and cleaning up before she headed back home.

When she left, I took a shower and waited for my
brothers to get home. I was literally surrounded by men
at all times of the day. I didn't mind Hakeem living with
us, but it was slightly awkward because he had a thing
for walking around the house half naked. My knees for
weak every time. Not to mention, he had begun to look at
me funny. I couldn't quite put my finger on, but there
was something strange about him now.

Once they all got home, we ate dinner, dessert, and even
drank a couple bottles of Moscato.

While they sat in the living room and discussed
basketball, I kissed each of them on the forehead and
went on to take a shower and go to bed. I sat in the bed
and began to read "The Counselor" by Garret Jordan, that
damn Ebony was something else. But I loved reading
about her life, some say it was based on a true story.

After I dozed off, I woke up and my house was peaceful
and quiet. I walked around the house, Rakim was sleep
in the bed, Hakeem was in his room, Devin was in the
guest room, and I'm guessing Deshaun had gone home. I
think he and Bri were becoming exclusive. But the
thought of my best friend and brother getting it on, made
my stomach hurt.

I fixed two glasses of water, one for Rakim's side of the
bed, and another to sit by Hakeem's. He was a major
work out freak so he loved when I did stuff like that.
Water and protein shakes was a big part of his daily
regime.

When I walked into Hakeem's room, he moaned lightly
and switched positions in the bed, but was still sleep. I

slowly walked towards the door, when it made a noise while I was slowly trying to open it.

"Tacara?" He whispered still half sleep..

"What the hell?" I thought to myself. "Tacara?"

How'd he know about her? I know that he and Rakim were close but he'd never tell him about Tacara. How'd he know who she was? I wanted to find out so I played along to see exactly how he knew my sister/ my split personality.

"Heyyyy..." I whispered.

"Dang baby, I missed you.. Why didn't you wake me up?" He asked me, assuming I was Tacara.

"You were sleeping so peacefully, I guess I just didn't want to wake you." I replied.

"That's never stopped you before." He replied with a smile and the sound of sleep in his throat.

"It hasn't?" I asked with confusion.

"Naw baby, I've been missing our talks..." He responded, sitting up in the bed exposing his entire chest. I almost melted. But my husband, his twin, was right in the other room.

"So what exactly do we do when I come in here?" I asked.

"Ummm we talk duh. I scoot over, you sit next to me and we just talk about life. You feeling okay?" He asked, looking at me suspiciously and moving my bangs out of my face.

"I'm fine, I'm fine... I just... Are you sure all we've done
is talked?" I asked one more time.

He chuckled.

"Chill baby, you're starting to sound like your sister. Yes,
just talk. I respect you and I've showed you that there's
more to life than just having sex. I guess that's why you
haven't been around as much. Destiny's taken care of by
my brother, so I guess that means I won't get to see you
as much.." He said sadly, and looking down.

"What's wrong? I'm still here Hakeem, but I guess you're
right. Since Destiny's safe, there's really no need for me."
I replied as Tacara.

"But what about us?" He replied and I backed up a little.

"Huh, us? Like me and you? What about us?" I asked
wondering what the hell he was talking about.

"Tacara, can I be honest with you?" He asked.

"Umm yeah, I guess." I replied.

"Tacara, to be honest, I've spent my entire life being a
dog. Treating women like shit. Never knowing how to
respect or have a decent conversation with one, until the
day I met you. Honestly, I think I'm falling in love with
you..." Hakeem whispered.

"Huh, how? I'm, I mean my sisters married to your twin
brother?!" I replied.

"I know, I know, it's confusing but I have to have you
Tacara!" He reached to kiss me and I backed away fast.

"What's wrong with you baby?" He asked, still talking to
me as if I were Tacara.

"Ummm... We're fine, but I better go before Rakim wakes up..." I replied.

"Wait, wait baby..." He tried to stop me, but I continued walking with my heart beating out of my chest.

I quietly got back in the bed with Rakim, as he kissed me and put his arm around me.

"Where you been baby?" He asked with sleep in his throat.

"Umm just, getting us some waters.. Go back to sleep baby..." I replied.

"Okay Mrs. Abdul." He replied before turning around to go back to sleep.

"Oh, and baby.." He whispered.

"Yea...?" I responded.

"I just wanted to tell you thank you for the late night talks you have with Hakeem some nights. As a child my mom used to have to do for him all the time.. I love you baby..." He replied.

My heart started beating fast and my eyes got huge in the dark. So he knew about these talks?

"No problem baby, I love you too now get some sleep..." I whispered.

"That damn Tacara," I thought to myself.

To be continued...

PART 27

"Fraternal Fantasy"

-Destiny

I woke up that next day thinking, "what in the entire hell was going on?" I was more confused than ever! The nerve of Tacara and Hakeem falling in "love?" How in the hell did they think that would work out?

This was actually pretty serious.

I got up from bed, put on my pajamas and started a huge breakfast for myself and the boys. One thing they adored about being at my house, were the fresh, home cooked meals I prepped on the daily. Hakeem had mentioned on numerous occasions how it reminded him of back home. And although I used to love pork, I'd become used to substitute turkey bacon and other non-swine meats. Even my brothers were catching on to the non-pork epidemic.

I went to the refrigerator and pulled out a carton of eggs, the gallon of milk, and a stick of butter. With everything in my hands, I used my right foot to close the door, and then it happened. My body hadn't felt this way in months. I dropped all the eggs to the floor, and felt my body become numb. The tips of my fingers began to tingle and I felt myself becoming lightheaded as I was fading away.... "Not now Tacara, please!"

It was too late. She was here.

"Tacara please don't do nothing stupid!" I said to myself.

-Tacara

"Chill Destiny..."

I picked myself up from the floor and by that time all 3 boys had come to my rescue. I must give it to Destiny that bitch had it made. Hakeem, Rakim, Devin, and Deshaun treated her like some type of royalty.

"Baby you okay?" Rakim said while helping me up and checking to make sure I didn't have any scratches or bruises.

"I'm fine." I said aggressively snatching my hand from him. I'm going to be honest, his touch gave me a gross feeling. I had fallen deeply in love with Hakeem, and I think it was becoming more obvious every day. Well, at least when I was around. Hakeem had a special touch and glow I had never seen on any man before him.

"So what you cooking, good looking?" Rakim asked, flashing all 32 of his shiny, white ass teeth.

Let's be clear, I wasn't about to cook. I am not Destiny!

"Ummm honey, I was going to but I'm actually not feeling so well. I think I'll just go lie down for a while. And I'm going to call in today... My stomach is really upset." I replied with a lie, but truth is, my stomach did feel kind of funny.

That would be perfect though! The only thing I could think about was spending some quality time with Hakeem, while Rakim and Deshaun were out of the house! I couldn't wait!

I lied in bed for a while, then Rakim brought me grilled cheese sandwich with some tomato soup. He was actually a really great guy, just not for me.

As soon as I heard Rakim's car door close, I hoped out of bed and was headed to Hakeem's room. I felt like a teenage school girl! I took off her hideous glasses, then the I hurried to brush my teeth, which I'm sure Destiny had already done, but I had to make sure because on these days Hakeem and I would bump and grind!

He knocked on their bedroom door softly.

I opened it and he squinted slightly, as if he wasn't sure if it was Destiny or me.

"It's me baby..." I replied kissing him softly on his lips.

"Damn, I've missed you so much..." He said, holding my sides and looking at me in my eyes.

"I missed you too, sorry I've been gone for a couple days, but I promise to make it up to you.." I kissed his hips and grabbed his dick through his black, basketball shorts.

He began to passionately kiss me, but then suddenly stopped.

"A couple of days? Baby we talked last night, you don't remember?" He asked.

"Huh, no we didn't.. Destiny's created some type of mechanism to keep me away. I'm not sure what it is, but it used to be easy for me to push through but not anymore. Our body is changing, and I'm not sure why." I replied.

"So, hold up wait, wait..." He shook his head and stood back. "I told you I loved you last night... You don't remember?"

"No baby, that wasn't me!" We both stood there with our eyes opened wide!

"Oh shit!" We said in unison.

"Fuck it, she was bound to find out anyway Hakeem, I can't hide the way I feel about you! You've changed me.

You've made me become a better woman, seriously!" I told him sincerely reaching out to kiss him again, but then he pushed me away softly.

"I can't do this, it's not right! I mean I know it's you Tacara, but sometimes I see you and I see my sister-in-law, and the wife to my brother. I wanna love you, just you. Not Destiny too..." He began to get sentimental and I could see the hurt in his eyes.

"But it is me! Look at me! We're just like you and Rakim! Identical, but different in so many ways!" I replied.

"I guess you're right," he explained.

"Baby, not now. Can you just make love to me.. Just for now, make love to me, okay." I kissed his lips, he lifted me into his arms, and we went into his room.

He kissed my entire body softly, from head to toe. I felt his lips glide all over my body. The passion felt so good, it made my entire body shake! He moved down to between my thighs and began to eat me out. I grasped his head and felt myself creaming inside his mouth. I could tell he was enjoying every minute of it from the sound of the slurps and him constantly repeating, "Mmmm" to himself as if I was serving him a full breakfast platter from between my legs.

After a few minutes, his door swung open!

"Aye nigga wake up! Let's go to the gym!" Devin yelled out!

He stopped suddenly, with my legs in the air, and he turned his head to see who it was walking in his room!

"Devin! What the fuck Bruh you can't knock?" He asked!

"Knock? Fuck you mean knock? Wait, is that?" Devin paused with a look of total confusion!

"Bubba it's not what you think!" I hurriedly replied, trying to cover up my exposed body parts.

"Like hell it's not! You're a married woman, what the fuck are you doing Destiny?!" He shouted out!

"Bubba I can explain, just listen!" I yelled out!

"Wait, what did you just say?" He asked raising one eyebrow.

"I can explain?" I replied.

"No before that, what'd you call me?" He asked.

"Bubba?" I replied, and his face became pale and lifeless, like he had just seen a ghost!

"Tacara? Is that really you?" He asked becoming choked up, I could see the tears forming in his eyes.

"Yes Dev, it's me." I replied wrapping myself in Hakeem's red, silk bed sheets.

Devin embraced me with a hug and we began to cry together.

"I had no idea this was real! All this time I thought it was just some crisis Destiny was going through, but it's really you isn't it? I can tell! I missed you so much Tacara!" He exclaimed with tears falling down his face.

"But wait, how'd you know the difference?" Hakeem asked, standing there with his dick still semi-hard, in his basketball shorts. But neither I nor Devin was bothered by his gorgeous physique.

"No one ever calls me Dev or Bubba, but Tacara." He responded.

"Aww Dev! Bubba I missed you so much!" I went to go hug him again and felt myself become sick!

"Oh shit!" Hold on!

I stood right in the middle of Hakeem's room and threw-up on his floor.

"Baby you okay?" Hakeem said patting my back!

I ran to the bathroom to finish throwing up. But it wasn't a normal stomach bug. It felt different!

-Destiny

The last thing I remembered was waking up to make breakfast but I had all of a sudden ended up in the bathroom puking my brains out!

I heard a knock at the door! I put my glasses on, and threw on one of Rakim's large t-shirts from the laundry basket!

"Tacara, you okay?" I heard Devin's voice say from the other side of the door. My heart began racing. No this bitch hadn't come in and brought Devin into the mix! Damn Tacara!

I opened the door, and pushed my glasses up closer to my face.

"Tacara?" I asked clueless staring at him and Hakeem.

"Oh shit... It's Destiny..." Devin replied.

"Look, we have to talk.." Hakeem said, before I turned around to throw up again.

"It'll have to wait..." I replied.

"Here." Devin handed me a glass of water.

To Be Continued...

PART 28

"Fraternal Fantasy"

-Destiny

After a few glasses of ginger-ale I was starting to feel a little better. Both Hakeem and Devin had left so I was left in the house alone to recuperate. I didn't know what was going on/wrong. But for some reason I could feel and sometimes even hear Tacara's thoughts.

My life was getting crazy, yet again.

A couple weeks had gone by and one night I finally decided to go talk to Hakeem once I knew Rakim was sleeping. I knocked on his door softly, so I wouldn't wake Rakim.

"It's open.. Come in..." He replied nonchalantly.

"Tacara?" He asked with a look of confusion.

"No, it's me Hakeem..." I replied pointing to my glasses on my face.

"What's up sis?" He sat up in the bed, exposing his upper body and moved over so that I could come sit next to him.

"We have to talk, it's kind of important..." I replied.

"I figured this was coming..." He replied.

"What do you mean?" I asked.

"You've been having morning sickness and calling into work every other day, you're pregnant aren't you? Does Rakim know?" He asked nervously.

"Not yet, I wanted to wait until after my doctor's appointment before I notified him. But there's something I need you to be honest about Hakeem."

"Anything sis... What's up?"

"Have you and...'Tacara' been sleeping together? Be honest..."

"I mean maybe once or twice, but I pulled out I promise! I knew the risk it would be had I nutted in you, I mean her." He replied, then took a sip of water.

"This is crazy... I don't know what to do? How are we going to explain this Rakim?!" I felt myself becoming emotional.

That's when Hakeem reached his hand to grab mine. I almost snatched away from him quickly but it felt comforting.

"Are you sure you never came in me?" I asked.

He looked down and then back up at me...

"Maybe once, but it was when Tacara and I first started talking. I'm sorry I liked D." He replied.

He made me feel safe and explained to me that we would all be in this together. He also tried to tell me that Rakim would be okay with it, but that was hard to believe.

"Ummm... Destiny, can I ask you something?"

"Yeah, what's up?"

"I really want to see Tacara tonight, is there a way you can make her appear." He asked seriously.

I chuckled lightly.

"It doesn't really work like that. She only comes when I'm in danger or turned on by the wrong person. It's complicated." I responded.

"So you're telling me, if I did this, she'd appear?" He asked reaching over to kiss my lips softly with his big juicy, luscious brown lips, and I felt my clit pulsating.

"No Hakeem, I don't think that work... Stop please..." My mouth was saying no but my body was screaming HELL YES!

He then lifted my t-shirt, kissed my breast slowly, and stuck his fingers down my panties. I wanted to say no but it honestly felt so good. I closed my eyes as his fingers entered me. I reluctantly moaned aloud!

"Shhhhh!" He said, covering my mouth with his masculine hands.

"Stop Hakeem this is so wrong..." I replied... Then I felt myself drift away... Damn it was actually working. I felt Tacara coming...

-Tacara

I took off her glasses and felt myself become angry.

"Hakeem don't play with me!" I snapped back.

"But I couldn't help it we have to talk..." He replied.

"About what?" I asked.

"Me, you, this, US!" He replied.

"Well now that you have me turned on, can you just fuck me before Rakim wakes up.. We can talk later.." I replied pulling my panties down, and grabbing his dick which was already hard as a rock.

"Shit, that's cool with me..." He whispered pulling down his black boxers and exposing his big dick.

I laid down on his bed and he climbed on top of me and entered me raw. It felt so good. Every inch. It was almost as if I could feel it in my stomach. I moaned lightly and he whispered sweet-nothings in my ear.

He began to drill me faster and the pleasure quickly turned into pain.

"Slowdown baby!" I whisper loudly, "calm down! Something doesn't feel right!"

"I'm about to cum though!" He replied with sweat dripping from his face! He began to pound me even harder!

"Hakeem something isn't right! Stop!" I yelled out! And I could hear Rakim getting up!

"Put on your clothes hurry up!" I whispered!

I stood up, and felt a sharp pain in my abdomen and fell to the floor!

"Tacara? Tacara? Baby?! Are you okay? Get up."
Hakeem panicked lifting my lifeless body from the floor
and putting my clothes back on before Rakim came in.

Rakim walked in with nothing but pajama bottoms on.

"DESTINY! Baby you okay?! What's wrong with her
Hakeem?" He said in a state of rage!

"We were just talking, like we do every night bro and she
passed out!"

"We got to take her to the hospital, let's go!"

They both lifted me and put me into the car.

I was unconscious, but shit was about to hit the fan!

To be continued...

PART 29

"Fraternal Fantasy"

-Destiny

     "Good morning baby girl, how you feeling?"
Rakim said as I opened my eyes finally. There was a
strange, misty fog over my eyes, so I could barely see
anyone in the room. But I felt Rakim's touch and I knew
his pleasant voice.

"Morning Rakim, what happened?" I asked hoping to God he didn't know the truth, believe it or not. Tacara and I spoke more than ever now, it felt something like a dream most of the time, but we were definitely learning to live as one in the same body.

"Well baby you were talking to Hakeem, and passed out. That's all we know so far. The other information is confidential but I'll go get the doctor, he assured me everything was fine though." Rakim responded with a smile on his face.

He was such a good man, I feared how he would handle all of this.

"Rakim wait, where are my glasses?" I asked.

"Baby, I'm not sure, for some reason you weren't wearing them when you passed out." He replied, almost as if he was insinuating something.

After a few minutes the doctor came in the room. My vision was blurry but I could see the doctor, I knew Rakim was near, and there were 2 other people in the room. It's not like I'm totally blind, but I can't see or make out anything without my glasses on.

"Morning Mrs. Abdul, how are you feeling?" The doctor asked.

"I'm fine sir, just curious to what happened?" I asked and then quickly regretted the question after it slipped my lips.

"Well I have some confidential information I want to share with you but it's up to you whether you want your husband and brother in law in the room."

"Umm she's cool with it, we have no secrets, so what's up Doc!" Rakim said before I could even answer.

"Rakim, would you mind just stepping out for a second..."

"For the hell what? You're my wife, if something is wrong I need to be the first to know. So fuck that! What do you have to tell US Doctor?!" He said aggressively while making himself comfortable on the end of the hospital bed. He never cursed around me, I became nervous that he must have kind of had an idea of what was really going on.

"Ugh go ahead doctor, and Rakim watch your mouth..." I said as he sat there like a 6 year old who was happy that he'd just gotten his way.

"Well Mr. And Mrs. Abdul it appears that you're about 11 weeks pregnant..." The doctor said and my heart dropped.

Rakim and I were going on our third month of being married, but honestly the only time he nutted in me was the first night, which would have been 12 weeks ago. But neither one of us were sure how the whole pregnancy thing worked, but the smile on his face was to die for.

Hakeem and I looked at each other, with nervousness.

"Well that definitely explains the weight gain... Sorry baby, not to be rude but I was going to tell you to lighten up on the Krispy Kreme!" Rakim said and then started laughing! He kissed me on my forehead.

"Baby, I'm so happy!" He replied.

"Hey baby! I came as soon as Devin called me!" My mom came bursting in the doors with a pair of my glasses from high school. They didn't help much, but at least I could see everyone.

"Thanks momma..." I replied nervously.

"Well... What happened? What's wrong?" My mom shouted.

"I just found out I'm pregnant momma..." I replied and she became teary eyed!

"I'm going to be a grandmother! How far along are you?" She asked.

"I'm 11 weeks, and he's going to give me an ultrasound soon so we can make sure the baby is okay after last night." I replied.

"Doctor what exactly happened last night?" My mom asked.

"Well it's personal information ma'am but if your daughter is okay with me saying it in front of you all, I can." He replied nervously. My mom was very intimidating.

"Ummmm..." I was about to say ummm no! But my mom quickly interjected!

"I'm her mother. I sat in labor with her narrow ass and wiped her narrow ass, and raised her narrow ass. We have no secrets. Spill it!" She replied.

"Hmph" I thought to myself about the "secrets" comment she made.

"Well sex is fine during the later trimesters, but in certain cases it can be kind of risky in the beginning trimester. It seems that last night you may have taken it a bit too far.. You have to be care Mr. And Mrs. Abdul." He explained and I could see the look of confusion of Rakim's face.

"Wait what? And doctor she didn't pass out from sex? She was just....." He stopped in the middle of his conversation, I guess he had realized the truth. He looked at Hakeem with rage in his eyes!

"Wait, I can explain bro!" Hakeem hurriedly began to explain himself!

"Explain what mother fucker! Explain how you've been fucking my wife! Huh! Damn Hakeem! I give you everything. Since dad died I've carried you and taken care of you like your got damn father! But no more pack your shit and get the fuck out of my house!" Rakim was outraged. I had never heard him use some of those words.

"And you! How dare you Destiny! I've been so damn good to you! Why baby?! Why Hakeem?! What the entire fuck!" He looked at me with sadness in his eyes! "I would never cheat on you.. How could you do this to me?!"

"I can explain...." I replied before the lights began to flicker, the machines that I was hooked too began to flash on and off, and my sight was now 20/20. I was turning into Tacara.

-Tacara

"HAKEEM DON'T GO!" I said while taking off Destiny's glasses.

"Rakim listen. My sister nor your brother would ever hurt you. This is my fault." I explained.

"Oh really?! Here we go with this shit again! Cut the crap Destiny! You can't let this split personality bull shit make it okay for you to be a got damn hoe!" He said in a rage.

"Bro, she's not lying. That's Tacara you're talking to, not Destiny. Just look at her..." Hakeem said and I could see that Rakim was calming down.

"Fuck you mean? She looks like my wife!" He expressed.

"No Rakim, really look at her..." Hakeem said once more and Rakim took a closer look.

He took a few steps closer to me, moved my bangs from my face and looked into my eyes.

"This shit is insane. You really do look different from my wife. Your eye color is even different. Is this really real?" He said rubbing my face, and still gazing in my eyes with confusion.

"Yes Rakim, I'm not your wife sometimes. I really am Tacara." I explained.

"This is too much for me! I gotta go!" Rakim threw his hands up, and headed for the door!

"Rakim wait, there's more!" I yelled out before he walked out of the room.

"What is it now Destiny/Tacara?!" He said with anger and hurt in his voice.

"We're in love..." I replied while looking at Hakeem.

Rakim looked like he was about to explode, my mom looked like she was 4 seconds from a heart attack, and the doctor looked like he needed some popcorn because it was so interesting to him.

Things were really about to get crazy.

To be continued...

PART 30

"Fraternal Fantasy"

Rakim rushed out of the hospital room, with rage and went into the waiting room.

There was an older, black lady there, who was sitting a couple seats down from him.

She had grey hair, soft wrinkles, some black slide-on, 1 inch heels, with a shiny, royal blue, ball-room dress gown on. She looked like she was dressed to go out to a jazz nightclub, in the 60's.

Rakim put his head down to gather his thoughts about what's to come, when the older lady came over to sit by him.

"You okay baby?" She asked Rakim, gently placing her hand on his back.

It startled him but then he realized it was just a nice old lady.

"You scared me, but yes ma'am, I think I'll be okay.." He replied, forcing a smile. He didn't really want to be bothered, but was too respectful to be rude.

"You don't have to sugar-coat nothing for me baby, I raised 4 boys, I can tell when one is in pain. You wanna talk about it?" She asked.

"Honestly ma'am, talking about it would make me feel a lot better, but it'd be too much to even try to explain..." Rakim replied then took a deep breath.

"Well just try me.. I have nothing but time.." She replied.

Rakim looked down the hospital hallways and then back at the lady. It seemed as if it were just the two of them in the entire hospital.

"Well my wife is suffering from a mental illness, it's some type of multiple personality, or some people call it D.I.D, Dissociative Identity Disorder. And ma'am, I was okay with that. I really tried to be. But things have gotten out of hand." Rakim said sadly.

"How so?" The lady asked.

Rakim thought to himself how crazy he must have sound to be explaining his life story to a complete stranger but he continued anyway.

"She just found out she was pregnant. And ma'am, my father died at a young age, so I've always wanted a child to love and nurture. The few years I had with my dad were amazing, and I just want to provide that love to my own baby boy or girl someday." He replied.

"So what's the problem?" The lady asked.

"It's her spilt personality. She's been sleeping with my brother or something. I know its confusing ma'am, and might sound outlandish, but..." He paused.

"But what baby?" She asked.

"I've been going on and on about my problems and I haven't even asked who are you or what you're doing here." He responded.

"I'm Phyllis Jones. I'm here visiting my husband. We've been married for 58 years, and we go dancing every Friday night. No matter what. But he too suffers from a mental illness. So sometimes, it puts a slight damper on our plans." She replied and Rakim became captivated.

"Really? Do you mind if I ask what is it he suffers from?" Rakim asked anxiously.

"He was diagnosed with Hypomanic episodes, which is a form of Bi-polar disorder. Some days Jeff wakes up and doesn't even remember who I am, but I'll spend as many hours as it takes to remind him that I'm his wife. His mood swings were so bad at times, we would have to admit him into the hospital for days at a time. As he got older, it got worse. It caused Dementia, memory loss, when we were in our 40's." She replied.

"And you still stuck around, even after all of that?" Rakim asked.

"Oh yes baby. See, my Jeff is my everything. I knew of his disorder before I married him, but I love and cherish him even till this day. My bones may be brittle, my back may hurt from sitting here for hours, but my heart still beats just for him. And whether he's up for it or not, I still get dressed up so we can go dancing." Ms. Phyllis explained and Rakim let the words she was saying sink in.

He was realizing that even through all this mess and confusion, Destiny needed him. For the first time he was realizing that his love for her outweighs any illness or disorder.

"Mrs. Jones, you have no idea how much it meant for me to run into you tonight. I needed this talk so bad, thank you... Would it be weird if I asked for a hug?" Rakim asked.

"Honey, I would've been offended if you didn't give me one... Now come here." She said opening her arms to embrace Rakim with a tight hug.

"Now go down there and fix this with your wife! Her and that baby need you! Go on now." She said while shooing him away.

"Yes ma'am..." Rakim replied. "And you and Mr. Jeff have fun tonight when y'all go dancing."

"We always do baby, we always do."

He walked down the hallway and said a quick prayer before entering back into the room where everyone was. As soon as he opened the door, the doctor was about to leave.

"Mr. Abdul, we were just talking about you. Your wife is good to go, I'll need to see her in about a week for some extra testing..." The doctor announced. The rest of the family had gone.

"Thanks Doc..." Rakim replied and then shook his hand.

"Hey Doc, can I ask you something real quick?" Rakim whispered to the doctor in the doorway.

The doctor turned around.

"Yes Sir Mr. Abdul?"

"The lady in the waiting room right there, which room is her husband in? I understand if you can't tell me. But I just really wanted to visit him sometimes. Not to be weird, but that lady and I just found out we have a lot in common..." The doctor had a strange look on his face, squinted his eyes, and then peered down the hallway to see who Rakim was referring to.

"Are you referring to Mr. Jeffrey Jones? Miss Phyllis's husband?" The doctor asked looking back at Rakim.

"Yes sir, that's him. Which room is he in?" He asked again.

"Sorry to tell you son, but Mr. Jones died 4 years ago. Yet, Miss. Phyllis still comes here every Friday night as if she's waiting on us to tell her he's back. She wears that same dress every Friday. After a few hours, she goes home. But she's never missed a Friday. That's what you call true love..." The doctor responded, then patted Rakim on his shoulder. "I'll see you and your wife next week."

Rakim peeked down the hallway and Ms. Phyllis was gone. He entered all the way in the room and there was no one else in there. Just me sitting on the hospital bed with my glasses on.

"Rakim, I understand if you don't want to continue with this marriage. I'll have my things out of the house by the morning time." I wiped the tears from my left eye.

Rakim pondered on what he and Miss. Phyllis had just discussed.

"You're not going anywhere baby. For better or worse, remember? Through sickness and through health? Remember?" Rakim asked, and then sat by me on the bed.

"I love you Ms. Destiny. And I want to spend the rest of my life with you, no matter what." Rakim replied.

"you promise?" I asked.

He stood up, then held out his hand.

"Let's go home baby..." Rakim replied.

To be continued..

PART 31

"Fraternal Fantasy"

When we pulled up to the house, we noticed my brother Deshaun moving some large boxes into his truck. We pulled in the driveway, and I got out to see what was going on.

"Sup little sis, you good huh?" Deshaun asked while embracing me with a hug and a kiss on the forehead.

"Yeah, I'm fine.. What's the boxes for?" I asked while rubbing my stomach. I'm not sure why, but I had just found out I was pregnant a few hours ago, but it seemed to enhance my motherly instincts already.

"Well, ummm I think Hakeem's probably going to be staying at my crib until he figures things out.." Deshaun replied as Hakeem was walking out of the front door.

"Keem you're not going anywhere, put the boxes up. We're not doing this dramatic scene crap. You hear me?" Rakim forcefully spoke to Hakeem.

"First of all: Who you talking to like that? You better pump your breaks." Hakeem replied with a look of disgust on his face.

"Did I miss something? Shouldn't I be the one mad?" Rakim replied.

"I guess so Rakim, but everyone has acknowledged your feelings, Destiny's feelings, but damn, what about mine?"

Hakeem replied, trying to sound tough, but I could hear his voice emotionally cracking.

"Destiny can you and Deshaun give us a minute? Please." Rakim looked at my brother and I, as we stepped over the boxes and made our way inside to give them some privacy.

"Your feelings Keem? Your feelings? Do you know how many times a day I take into consideration 'your feelings,' do you have any idea how much I stress over you and your damn feelings?! Huh! Look at me when I'm talking to you bruh!" Rakim said.

"I know, I know. I'm a huge burden to everybody! Right? I don't do shit right! Huh? I'm just your fucked up twin brother huh?" Hakeem replied sadly.

"Keem I'm not doing the personal pity party crap with you today! Okay?! I didn't say you're a burden, I just said I worry about you more than anybody else on this planet. I pray for you, more than I pray for myself! You mean the world to me dude. Now, don't get me wrong, some shit has gotten a little out of hand. But it was nothing any of us could've ever anticipated. So let's unpack these boxes, grab a bottle of some cheap liquor and figure this shit out. We have a baby to raise." Rakim replied, and Hakeem gave him the most genuine look of despair.

"We?" Hakeem asked.

"Yes, WE, me, you, Destiny.... And Tacara. WE have to figure this out and WE have to give this baby the world. You understand?" He grasped the back of Hakeem's neck, and pulled him towards him to give him a hug.

Hakeem started to tear up.

"So wait, what happens now?" Hakeem asked.

"We continue living the way we have..." Rakim replied.

"What about me and Tacara?" Hakeem asked.

"We'll figure it out..."

They both walked inside and I could tell from the looks on their faces that their conversation had to have been emotional.

"Sooooo... What did we decide?" I asked hesitantly.

"If it's cool with you sis, I would like to stay here with you and Rakim, and help raise the baby." Hakeem said politely.

"That's cool with me," I kissed him on the cheek for reassurance of our platonic relationship.

"So what about all these damn boxes?" Deshaun asked with one eyebrow raised.

"You trying to help us unpack them real quick?" Hakeem asked him.

"Man hell naw! I'm hungry as hell. I'm about to bounce, I'll holla at y'all later on." Deshaun replied jokingly.

"Shoot, on the real I'm kind of hungry too." Hakeem replied.

"Me too, Waffle House?" Rakim asked holding his hands out implying the question to all of us.

"Yep."

"Let's go."

"I'll drive."

Rakim reached over the seat to grab my hand, while he was driving.

As I sat down in the car, I realized that this entire dysfunctional mess actually made me happy.

My phone rang, and the caller I.D. said "Dr. Drew."

"Hello." I answered.

"Morning Destiny, its Dr. Drew. I have somethings I need to discuss with you, do you have a minute?" She asked.

"Yes ma'am," I replied turning down the radio, and holding my left hand up to imply to the boys to be quiet. "I'm listening..."

"First let me congratulate you on the pregnancy, yes your mom called and told me. But there are certain risk we must discuss in preparation of this pregnancy term." Dr. Drew responded.

"I know, I have a doctor's appointment coming with Dr. Harris next week." I replied.

"That's fine, but there's mental risk we must discuss as well. Can you make it in tomorrow morning?" She asked and I felt my heart racing. Mental risk? I thought to myself.

"Umm yes, that's fine. I'll be there." I replied.

"Okay, and make sure Tacara is there too...." Dr. Drew said.

"Ummm okay."

To be continued...

PART 32

"Fraternal Fantasy"

-Tacara

As soon as I woke up I could feel that something wasn't right. To be honest, I'd never really appeared unless it was a crisis or intimate moment, so why was I here now?

I got up from the bed slowly, attempting not to wake Rakim. But it didn't work.

"Baby?" He asked with the morning sun peeping through the blinds and gently kissing his dark skin.

I shook my head "no..."

"Tacara?" He asked with a sudden look of disappointment.

"Yeah, hey Rakim. Look, I'm not really sure why I'm here right now, but I am. So.... Don't we have a doctors appointment or something today?" I asked.

"Yeah we do. And I think that's why you're here. Dr. Drew made your sister pretty paranoid after a phone call yesterday. So she didn't get much sleep, every time I peeked over at her, she was wide awake. So I knew I'd be waking up to you. There's just certain things I'm not sure how to deal with, and so she still seeks you for protection." Rakim responded.

He was such a gentleman. Not many men could deal with a female with what Destiny has going on. But he's definitely embraced it.

"Aww thanks Rakim, you always make me feel welcomed." I replied.

"No problem, but can I ask you something?" Rakim's voice lowered to a whisper.

"Sure." I looked left to right, and whispered back to him.

"Have we ever had sex?" Rakim asked. "You know, like me and 'you?'"

"No, hell no. That's a volition of the sister code that Destiny and I share. Don't get me wrong, you're one of the greatest men on earth, but so is Hakeem." I replied with a smile.

"Mmm. Okay. Well go wake his black ass up and tell him to get ready. I feel like he should be there too." Rakim said eagerly.

"Okay.."

I took of Destiny's bifocals and sat them on their dresser. I swear I couldn't understand how she was blind as a bat, but I have 20/20 vision. If nothing else proved I was real, that certainly did.

I knocked on Hakeem's room door softly then let myself in.

"Keem..." I whispered. "Keem..."

He was laying on his back with his right hand behind his head, and the covers only covering his lower abdomen and thighs. I seriously tried to resist the temptation but I couldn't. I know with what just happened the other night, that it would be bad to have sex with him. So I figured I'd just taste it.

After I whispered his name, he still hadn't woke up. So I gently caressed his dick through the sheets and heard him begin to moan in his sleep.

He slowly opened his eyes, as soon as his dick entered my mouth.

"Good morning baby, damn..." He whispered loudly. "Slowdown."

The fact that 80% of men couldn't handle morning head because of the sensitivity, turned me on. It never fails, he'll always cum faster in the morning, than at night.

I felt his pre-cum gazing my throat, then I heard Rakim walk in.

I immediately picked my head up, but neither of them said anything. I figured the first time Rakim witnessed Hakeem and I in action, there would be a problem.

But it was the complete opposite.

"My bad." Rakim replied as if I didn't look identical to his wife.

"You good bruh, what's up?" Hakeem responded nonchalantly as if his dick wasn't standing at full attention.

What kind of freaky shit do they have going on? I thought to myself.

"We'll be ready in a minute..." Hakeem said, as Rakim slowly shut the door still starring as if he was completely turned on.

"What was that about?" I asked Hakeem.

"We have an agreement, like an understanding of how this works..." He replied with confidence.

"Oh really? And does Destiny know about this 'agreement?'" I said holding up my fingers to imply quotation marks.

"Yeah, she does actually. I mean, think about. It's every twin boys' dream to date twin sisters. In some strange way, that's what we're doing." He replied and it made perfect sense.

"Hmph, I guess that does make sense." I replied.

"Now can you finishing sucking me up?"

To be continued...

PART 33

(2 months later)

-Destiny

Things couldn't be any better. It's the summer time and my little family just seemed to be working out.

Turns out, I'm having twins. But I'm sure you probably seen that coming.

Tonight we're having a barbecue and Devin decides there was something he needed to discuss with the family.

Rakim and Hakeem woke up around 10AM and I could hear them laughing and joking while prepping the meat for the grill.

"What are y'all doing? Doesn't smell like cooking yet and I'm starving." I replied rubbing my baby bump. I had just made 19 weeks, the day before. So they guys were totally intrigued on knowing the sexes of the babies.

Dr. Drew channeled a way for Tacara and I to speak to each other whenever. I know, it seems crazy. But it works.

"Give us a couple hours baby, you want a turkey sandwich until then?" Rakim asked as I walked into the kitchen.

"Umm yeah baby, that actually sounds pretty good." I replied.

"Yeah, let me get one of those too bruh." Hakeem replied.

I made myself a glass of orange juice and sat down at the kitchen table to watch them prepping.

Hakeem and Rakim had a bond a lot like Devin and Deshaun.

I took a shower, picked out some comfortable clothes for myself and Rakim and made my way to the back patio where my family was.

"Sis I can't believe you're having twins!" Devin exclaimed with a look of excitement.

"I know, but last night I was starting to think of how crazy it would've been to only be raising one child. Don't you think?" I asked.

"I guess... You know, some people do only have 1 child at a time. Outside of mom and Mrs. Abdul." Devin leaned down and kissed my stomach. "But I'm so glad we're having 2! Cheers!"

He held up his wine glass, then remembered I couldn't drink.

"Cheers..." I said, holding up a cold cup of water.

Once the nightfall came, I went inside a little while before everyone else to take a shower. And check on Devin. With all the new changes my body was going through, a quick shower just felt warm, clean and normal. And I had guessed earlier Devin was having some new relationship dilemma because he seemed distant.

I got inside, closed the slide door and was headed down the hallway. I heard Devin talking on his phone in Hakeem's bathroom!

"I don't know how much longer I can do this!" He whispered loudly into his phone.

"What do you think I'm talking about, this fucking charade! I can't do it anymore!" He got louder into the receiver.

"Has anyone took a second to think about the actual babies that are about to be born into this! We need to do something momma! This can't be right!" Devin was becoming hysterical.

"They need to be admitted momma! And those babies need to be given to a normal family!" He urged!

"They're not fucking twins momma!" Devin yelled.

I pushed the door open!

"Devin! What's wrong with you?" I shouted across the bathroom almost in tears.

"Destiny, not right now! I'm just going to go home!" He began to walk past me!

-Tacara

"No! It's not fucking Destiny, so sit your sissified-punk ass down somewhere! Now!" I yelled to him, and he stopped in the middle of his tracks.

He turned around and gave me a cold look, one I'd never seen from him before.

I could tell my words took him back to a dark place.

"What did you just call me?" He asked with a harsh tone and look of deceit.

"Sissified? Punk ass? Or bitch?" I counted them out with my fingers as I said them aloud.

"You didn't say bitch." He replied.

"Well I meant too." I closed the door and wobbled more into the bathroom.

"Do you know how many times I had to help you up from getting your ass beat by dad? Do you have any idea how many times he verbally abused you a day! He knew you were gay, long before you or anyone else did Devin! And tried to literally beat it out of you on a daily basis! You would scream, and cry! But he would just tell us to 'pray' for you! We weren't allowed to ask why you were getting brutally bashed! But the only person with some compassion over your situation, lifestyle, whatever the fuck you want to call it! Was Destiny! I don't understand it, dad damn sure couldn't handle it, and let's be honest! Deshaun tolerates it! But Destiny is the one family member you can confide in! Don't fucking ruin her opportunity to feel some sense of normalcy! You wouldn't want anyone to take that from you!"

I preached to Devin, and I could tell it made him understand better.

-Destiny

"Why are you crying Dev? What's wrong?" I kneeled down to the floor and held him closer to me.

"Whatever it is, just tell me..." I said while rubbing his hair.

"I knew something was bothering him." I thought to myself

To be continued.

PART 34

"Fraternal Fantasy"

-Destiny

A few months had gone by and the house had become totally desolate. My raging hormones made me feel so alone! Everyone that was important to me, had slowly been pushed away. But it wasn't my fault. Devin and Deshaun only came around to spend time with the other brothers, so most of the time I just read to myself. I couldn't wait until my babies were here. Then at least I wouldn't feel so alone.

I wobbled into Dr. Drew's office and sat down on her chaise to begin our therapy session.

"How are you feeling?" Dr. Drew asked as she positioned her hands together then placed them directly in front of herself.

"Fat..." I rubbed my belly. "Very fat. Is my mother coming today?"

"She is," Dr. Drew glanced at her watch, "just late as usual. Why is there something you maybe wanted to discuss while it's just the two of us?"

"Kind of. If that's okay." I replied.

"I insist. Tell me what's going on."

"Lately, I've just been feeling left out. It's almost as if no one cares to be seen around me. And when I am there, it's like I'm the huge elephant in the room that everyone is discussing how to kill." I replied.

"I'm sorry you feel that way, is there anything that may have been said to make you feel that way?" She asked with concern.

"No, not to me, but of course everyone speaks their opinion to Tacara... But I haven't been able to see her in days?" I replied.

"See her?" Dr. Drew asked. "As in a reflection or someone else standing in the room?"

"I mean, it's just my reflection but it's so different when she's present. My glasses are redundant when she's around, and there's this huge relief of anxiety and pressure, I can't really explain it. But, she told me something, but I don't know if I should say it." I replied.

Dr. Drew paused for a moment.

"Did you tell your mother yet?" Dr. Drew asked.

"Not yet, but I plan to today."

"What did Tacara tell you that you weren't so sure about?" She asked.

"It wasn't so much to what she said, as to what I saw." I hesitated.

"What was it? What'd you see?" She asked harshly!

"Bruises. And I fear that since she is a part of me that she and Hakeem's relationship could be harmful to me and the babies." I responded.

"You're exactly right Destiny, something must be done. Did you tell Rakim?"

"No ma'am, but I plan to show him tonight." I replied.

"Dr. Drew, my brother Devin said something that kind of made me wonder the other day." I said aloud.

"Okay, about what?" She asked.

"He made a comment about someone 'not being twins' was he referring to me and Tacara or someone else." I asked.

"Well, he definitely wasn't referring to you nor Tacara. But," Dr. Drew began to speak but then paused.

"But what? Who was he referring to then?" I asked.

"Let me put it this way, since the first day I met you, you've always been a really understanding person. I'll just say, don't let your love, compassion and understanding get in the way with what is actually standing in front of you.." Dr. Drew replied and I was totally confused. But I just shook my head and said ok.

After the therapy session my mom took me out to eat for lunch and then home. It was simple, and none-loving, almost as if she didn't really want to be bothered with me. Something was wrong, and I could feel it happening around me. Everybody was keeping something from me, but what was it?

Once I got home Rakim was waiting in the living room, in the dark. I walked through the front door and was immediately greeted by the sweet smells of cinnamon and vanilla. It was perfect and made me feel warm.

I flipped the switch to turn the lights on.

"Rakim, what's wrong with you?" I asked looking at him like he was crazy.

"I'm losing my mind baby." He responded with his hands covering his eyes, as if he had been crying. "I'm losing my fucking mind baby."

I got closer to him to embrace him.

"Why you say that, what happened?" I replied.

"I almost killed my brother today! Like, literally killed him D!" He replied, and that's when I noticed the purplish bruises around his neck.

"What? What happened?! Where is he?" I got up quickly to search the house for Hakeem!

"Tacara told me what happened, she told me he's been abusing her!" Rakim yelled out!

I ignored what he was saying, and was still searching the house for Hakeem!

"Where's Hakeem? Rakim. Please tell me you didn't do anything you'll regret later!" I shouted!

"He's fine.. He just went out, but he's okay." Rakim replied and then gave me an indifferent look.

I went into my bathroom to call my mother. I thought it would be a good idea for me to stay with her for the remainder of my pregnancy. Which would only be a few more days. I honestly felt like this house was becoming a bit too much for me.

I stopped at the sink to catch my breath, and hold my stomach for a second.

As I gathered my stuff together, I looked through the halls and Hakeem was standing there with the exact bruise marks as Rakim around his neck.

"Hakeem, I heard what happened, are you okay?" I asked, trying not to make eye contact with him, but he didn't respond.

"Keem?" I said his name again. "Keem are you okay?!"

He didn't say anything.

I walked into the living room with my bags packed.

"Destiny what the hell is this, where are you going?" Rakim looked at my bags and got upset.

"I just want to go stay at my mom's until the baby comes." I replied.

"You weren't going to ask me? What in the hell did I do wrong?" Rakim shouted then took a sip of his Whiskey & Coke mixture.

"Nothing, I just need a few days of peace and quiet. I'm fine baby, I just want to go to my mom's house for a few days. Calm down, you didn't do anything wrong." I replied in a mellow tone.

I turned around and headed for the kitchen to fix myself some water before my mom got there. I propped the refrigerator door opened with my foot, then slowly poured me some water and took a sip from it.

I closed the refrigerator door and there was Hakeem standing there with something in his hand.

"Keem what are you....?" I paused.

"BOP!"

He knocked me out and put a split in the middle of my forehead. As he drug my lifeless body through our house, I felt like I needed to scream but couldn't convince the words to come out! I attempted to grasp the carpet or door frame but I was way too weak!

He grabbed under my arms, and proceeded to drag me down the steps and into the basement. After a few minutes he put tape over my mouth, and gently tied my hands behind my back. It's weird, I didn't really feel like my life was in danger, I felt like I was apart of some sick joke.

There was a knock at the door.

"My mom?" I thought to myself.

I heard his footsteps go to open the door, and she was frantic.

"Where's Destiny?" She rushed brushed past him in the doorway and proceeded to look for me.

"I haven't seen her, I thought she was still with you." Hakeem answered.

I tried to moan and scream but the compression from the tap across my mouth wouldn't let the words come out!

"Wait, I thought you moved out?" My mom asked.

"Of my own house? Why would I do that? No ma'am, now let me go ask Hakeem if he's seen Destiny." Hakeem responded.

"But you are Hakeem? Aren't you?" My mom asked confusingly.

"Ah yes ma'am, I meant Rakim. I do that from time to time." He answered and walked away immediately.

My mom looked to the left and seen that my bags were sitting next to the door.

"Destiny! Destiny?! Baby its momma! Where are you?" She shouted through the house, as tears began falling from my face because I had no way to tell her where I was!

She began to call my phone. As it began to ring in her ear, the actual phone began to ring from Hakeem's pocket.

"Why do you have her phone?" My mom asked.

"Honestly, I'm not even sure why I have it." He responded.

"And what happened to your neck..?" She asked as she backed up slowly towards the door.

My mom decided to call the police just to be on the safe side, she felt like things were getting out of hand.

To be continued.

PART 35

Once the police got there I heard them asking a lot of questions!

"I told you already, the last time I seen her she was leaving to go with her mom's house!" Hakeem responded.

I heard one of the officers walking down the basement stairs and I began to kick my feet to make noise and let him know I was down stairs.

"I think I got something!" The young officer yelled out.

"Destiny? Is it my baby?" My mom yelled out following closely behind him.

As the young officer proceeded towards me slowly, with a flashlight in one hand and a gun in the other, I thought about how much trouble Hakeem would get in and the strain it would cause Rakim for stressing over him. I wiggled my hands through the ropes and removed the tape from my mouth, just in time before the officer's flashlight hit my face.

"Destiny?" He called out.

"Yeah it's me! I'm sorry, I fell and no one could hear me! I'm fine though, I'm fine, can you just come help me up!" I replied. I heard my mom running down the stairs!

"Is that her! Is that my baby?!" She came down the stairs and horridly embraced me with a tight hug! She snatched the flashlight away from the officer and pointed it all over my body.

"Baby what happened? Who hit you in the head? Are you okay?" She ran her hands across my body to see if I had any other bruises or scars.

"I'm fine momma, I'm fine. I fell and no one could hear me screaming. But I'm okay. Can you help me up?"

As her and the officer helped me to my feet, I made eye contact with Rakim in the stairwell, he looked as if he had just seen a ghost.

I took one step up the stair and felt a rush of water going down my legs.

"My water just broke..." I said and everyone began to panic, even the officers.

The contractions began almost suddenly! I felt like I was carrying two bowling balls around!

"Come on baby! Let's go!" Rakim yelled as we headed for the front door!

"Grab my bags please, and somebody call the hospital!" I yelled out. "And call my brothers!"

"I'll lead the way!" The officer yelled out.

I nervously got into the car with Rakim, and we were in route to the hospital. I was attempting to concentrate on my breathing, but I had to ask Rakim this question.

"Where's Hakeem?" I asked.

"Listen baby, there's something I need to tell you about Hakeem..." Rakim said sadly!

-did he kill him? I thought to myself.

"What? What happened?!" I asked loudly as he became nervous.

Right as he was about to speak I got a sharp pain in my lower stomach, it felt like a midget was stomping on my lower abdomen with timberland boots on!

"He ummm...." Rakim paused.

"Wait! Wait..." I held his arm and the door handle until the pain went away.

We pulled up to the hospital and there was my brothers, a nurse with a wheelchair, and I think Hakeem was standing right behind them. But I wasn't sure.

Devin opened my car door with the biggest smile on his face!

"You ready sis?! Let's do this!" He exclaimed with excitement.

I answered a few questions for the nurse and then they laid me down. My contractions were back to back, but the only thing I could think about was the fact that I was about to give birth to twins, and my husband may have been a murderer!

"I'm going to push!" I yelled out to the nurse!

"You can't! The doctors not here! Wait! You can't start pushing yet!" Nurse Tiffany responded!

"She's ready to push ma'am, the twins are coming now!" Rakim yelled out to her!

He grasped my left hand and I closed my eyes! All of a sudden I looked to the right and there was Hakeem! I had the biggest smile on my face!

Hakeem!" I smiled, and looked at Rakim who had a sad look on his face.

"Hakeem's not here Destiny..." Rakim replied.

"But he's right here, look..." I replied.

Rakim looked over to my right side and just put his head down.

"Hakeem doesn't exist Destiny. He's just like Tacara. You and I both suffer from multiple-personality-disorder, Hakeem died in a car accident with my dad, he's gone baby..." Rakim responded and I felt my cervix opening up to its full extent.

I began to think about all the times I had "met" or "encountered" Hakeem, and the vision of him slowly faded away. Hakeem was Rakim.

I heard the doctor telling me to push and I could feel my babies leaving my womb, but the only thing I could think about was all the memories I shared with Hakeem. And in reality it was just Rakim.

I looked around the hospital room and there was Rakim, holding my left hand, my mom sitting on the sofa, Tacara and Hakeem both on my right side.

Tears began to fall from my face.

"Push sis! Push!" Tacara and Hakeem said in unison.

That night I gave birth to a beautiful baby girl, and a handsome baby boy. Hakeem Raylen Abdul and Tacara Raynae Abdul.

I guess you can call it life after death.

THE END.